CHRISTIANITY BROKEN

D. K. GROOMS

iUniverse, Inc.
Bloomington

Christianity Broken

iUniverse books may be ordered through booksellers or by contacting:

iUniverse
1663 Liberty Drive
Bloomington, IN 47403
www.iuniverse.com
1-800-Authors (1-800-288-4677)

ISBN: 978-1-4620-4023-0 (sc)
ISBN: 978-1-4620-4024-7 (hc)
ISBN: 978-1-4620-4025-4 (ebk)

Library of Congress Control Number: 2011913262

Printed in the United States of America

iUniverse rev. date: 08/04/2011

CHRISTIANITY BROKEN

CONTENTS

FOREWORD

I have always wondered what motivates people to read the books they do, especially those who truly want to understand and know more about their Christian faith. Is it simple curiosity that drives them? A lot of people are certainly curious, or is there something within them that they can't quite put their hand on?

It is unusual to find a person today who longs to know more about the deep things of faith and the God they serve. These people, it seems, have a spiritual itch that desperately needs to be scratched. You'll find them reading everything they can get their hands on, that they feel might help satisfy their searching and longing soul. These people have heard countless messages and untold teachings on the ways of God, but for them the glass still remains half full. "Where do I go next?" they ask.

Having so many questions, but getting so few answers, these people feel frustrated in their search for truth, yet they know there must be answers somewhere. Their spirit senses their longing and encourages them to keep looking, that the answers are well within reach. The Word of God says in Matthew 5:6, "Blessed are they which do hunger and thirst after righteousness: for they shall be filled." What a wonderful promise for you and me. It also proclaims in 1 Corinthians 2:9-10, "But as it is written, Eye hath not seen, nor ear heard, neither have entered into the heart of man, the things which God hath prepared for them that love him. But God hath revealed them unto us by his Spirit: for the Spirit searcheth all things, yea, the deep things of God." It clearly states that we human beings can know the deep things of God, here and now.

Being hungry spiritually is a driving force that can be fulfilled only if we trust God to lead us to the source of refreshing. Man cannot lead you there—only God can. So, if you are one of "those people," or you feel compelled to find truth, no matter what it takes, then this might be just the book for you.

Sadly, most church members honestly believe the church is just fine the way it is, in spite of noticeable shortcomings. But you'll have to decide for yourself. You may well be surprised at what you'll learn by reading this book. It may unlock the mysteries you've been seeking answers to.

When I sought the Lord for an appropriate title for this book, I felt impressed by him to call it *Christianity Broken*. Without question, I knew in my heart of hearts that this was indeed the perfect title, but one which would no doubt cause serious controversy among believers. My hunger and zeal to see captives made free is my only purpose in writing this book. It's because of my unconditional love for the body of believers—"God's church"—that I even considered such an undertaking. But God's word to me to write this narrative was reason enough. He knows you are seeking and wants to reveal himself to you. That can only happen because of love.

Over the past several years, there have been some very distressing and sobering issues that I felt were being ignored in favor of doing business as usual. The church is my family, and I want them to understand the truth of the church's complacency in light of God's word. I now understand that the church is badly broken. Only when we individually and collectively accept that things are broken will we make any effort to correct those problems. Unfortunately (and perhaps profoundly), the church would argue just the opposite. In the eyes of the average Christian, they're convinced that everything is fine.

Considering these critical issues, it's my hope that you will indeed read the book through completely, that you'll be challenged and changed by what you read. The result will be a newer life in Christ and with the Father. After all, isn't that really what you wanted anyway?

This book is all about freedom. Freedom that will cause such a restlessness to arise within you that you'll not be content until you possess every last bit of his glory. If you read it, you'll be changed by it. I guarantee it!

Preface

A) Some tips for reading this book:

There's a tremendous amount of information in this book, and it can seem somewhat overwhelming when you first read it. So I've got some tips to help you get the most out of this book.

Once you've read the book, put it aside for a couple of weeks and simply digest everything you've read. After a brief period of time, pick the book up again and reread it. This time, read each of the chapters independently of the others. Take time to look up the referenced scriptures in that specific chapter, reading and meditating on them so you'll have clarity. Read them till you understand the context of the chapter in which they are found. Spend quality time carefully considering the issues revealed to you. Ask the Holy Spirit to help you understand how these elements apply to you specifically.

Do this with regularity, and you'll find that the truths I've explained will take hold of your life and become real to you. Your relationship and intimacy with Jesus Christ and the Father will blossom and grow in ways you never thought possible. It'll be the most glorious and rewarding adventure of your life.

Remember, Christ does not want us to be ignorant of his word or the things that were done by him for our benefit. He is with you to help you be all that you can be.

B) THE IMPORTANCE OF UNDERSTANDING THE BIBLE, GOD'S WORD TO YOU:

It is really quite easy to misquote scripture these days, especially in light of the growing number of easy-to-read Bible translations we see on the book shelves. Correctly interpreting and studying passages of scripture is the responsibility of each one of us.

Casual readers of the Bible often find themselves confused because of these easy-to-read Bibles. Some of them are beneficial, especially for the new Christian, but not the serious student.

Serious study of God's word is encouraged, but there is a tremendous cost. The cost is in both time and effort. Nothing comes quickly or easily, regardless of the vocation. You have to have a serious longing in your heart to know the "deep things" of God, beyond what you hear in a traditional church setting, spiritual truths that *make* you free.

Beyond just wanting to understand what the Bible is telling us, you'll need to start by doing some serious digging. Get yourselves a version of the Bible that hasn't been watered down for "simplicity" or for easy reading's sake. I highly recommend the King James or New King James Version, with a companion *Strong's Concordance* and a book that interprets English into Greek. This will teach you the true meanings of the words you read, in the context of the passage you're studying.

Never pick out a single scripture verse and make up a story that sounds good using it. Read the verses before and after it to gain a proper perspective of the whole passage. The books of the Old and New Testaments were not written in the fashion we see in our Bibles today, with verses and chapters. The church added them to make it easier to read. They were written as letters to the various churches. A letter is not choppy, but should read easily, with the intent of the writer being quite understandable.

INTRODUCTION

Don't be deceived: the Christianity we've grown up with is in a very sad state today. What makes it sad is that most believers just don't believe it. Our Christianity is not the Christianity of our fathers and forefathers. We talk as though it is, but it is not. There are colossal differences from what our Christian forefathers knew and embraced as faith and what we call faith today. No one seems interested in discussing the issues of our faith that are flawed, nor do they desire to confront any problems that might alienate them from their friends in the church.

If you remember what you were taught in school, you'll know that Rome didn't fall in a single night. It was a progressive destruction that was so thorough it left Rome a mere shadow of itself and its former glory. Erosion that was so complete, it lulled people into believing the later glory of Rome was no different than its former glory. They *allowed* themselves to be deceived because it still felt good to them on the outside. Just like a frog in a pot of water, we too like the warm fuzzy feeling of our surroundings and hope nothing will change. Tragically, what we enjoy isn't really real or good for us. It's a death sentence to those that remain there too long.

When people finally wake up to the reality of what has been happening with their faith and the church they attend, they'll no doubt question God and wonder what on earth happened to them.

The Christianity we claim to love and pin our hopes on is in fact broken. Like Rome, the erosion of our faith has resulted in a devastation that's nearly complete. The former glory is gone. "But how can that be?" you say.

Countless Christians would argue that the Christianity they know isn't broken at all, but vibrant and alive, even during these tumultuous and troubling times. They'll tell you that church attendance, though in noticeably smaller numbers, is still proclaiming the Good News of the Gospel and doing good deeds in their communities for mankind. They might even argue that there's actually more unity today than there has been in previous years, especially among the various denominations. They'll point out that major efforts are being made on every front to bring cohesiveness to all "believers," and unity of faiths. To them, life seems good and God is pleased with their efforts.

Maybe the thought of a broken Christianity sounds blasphemous to you too; perhaps it stirs up a bit of anger. If you'll remember from scripture, such were the times when Christ spoke of similar issues. Didn't he challenge the thoughts of men concerning their faith and relationship with God? Weren't they the ones who steadfastly obeyed the laws they'd received through Moses? Didn't they have their religion down pat and perfected, believing God was thoroughly pleased with their performance? I'm sure they would argue in the affirmative.

Surely these "holy men," the Sanhedrin and Pharisees, thought to themselves, "How dare this Jesus stand in opposition to the church of God and the religious practices we have grown to love?" These leaders of the "faith" were so angry they tried repeatedly to kill Jesus, to silence this perceived heresy. They hated the truth bearer. They hated what he represented. I wonder today if we too hate the truth?

Perhaps we should be more attentive to matters of our faith as God speaks of it in his word. Over the past many years, I have witnessed the ongoing deterioration and destruction of what we call Christianity. Everywhere I turn, I'm confronted with the reality of what has taken place. The things I read and hear shout loudly the truths of what has really happened to us. Satan, our professed enemy, has been quite effective in our world these past many years, specifically in the lives of Christian men and women and the churches they attend. He has successfully broken down and eroded our faith through a barrage of misinformation and lies concerning who we are in Christ and in this world. We all know that Satan is both a liar and deceiver; somehow believing we have him right where we want him. This hater of all things holy has been quite busy and effective in the Christian church as a whole. Satan has deceived multitudes about the true condition of the church. The result is predictable. Countless Christians still believe everything is fine.

I've witnessed this deterioration firsthand, both as a pastor and from outside the pulpit. As Christ wept bitterly over Jerusalem, so I too weep over a people separated from him. Scripture says in Luke 13:34, "O Jerusalem, Jerusalem, which killest the prophets, and stonest them that are sent unto thee; how often would I have gathered thy children together, as a hen doth gather her brood under her wings, and ye would not!"

Isaiah 41:9 says, "I have loved thee with an everlasting love."

My heart aches for the people of faith to have a clearly defined relationship with Christ. To this end, I find myself searching the Word of God to know the truths concerning this precious relationship with him. I seek his guidance continually, to know the depths to which he wants us to go in him. Is it possible to have the kind of relationship that Christ has with his father? To some that seems far fetched and unattainable, but his word claims it to be true to those who will seek him with their whole spirit, mind, and body. He also promised to reveal problems that we need to address if we're to have this unique relationship with him. I feel God specifically wants to address the many hindrances that restrict the flow of fellowship with his children, especially as it relates to broken relationships.

Brothers and sisters in Christ, we must be diligent in our faith, to know what is true and what is not. There is a heavy cost for enjoying the type of relationship that pleases God. But I tell you, it is worth the cost. Continually reflecting on the issues of our faith is the responsibility we must each embrace as we seek the face of God for ourselves, especially in the light of his glorious word.

During the past ten years, I've been made acutely aware of many troubling and disturbing things that are happening within the household of faith, both in our walk and the relationship with Christ and the Father. Things which, if left uncorrected or unchecked, will bring about a collapse of the glory we take so easily for granted.

My fervent study of scripture and my intense desire to know the fullness of Christ intimately has yielded a bountiful harvest of his truth. He has allowed me to see a great many falsehoods that are embraced by the church today. Misunderstanding or misinterpreting scripture alone has wreaked havoc with the lives of countless Christians. For this reason, I felt the call of God on my heart to put these concerns before the body of believers, in the form of this book, to identify the issues that should be of great concern for all believers. I also feel strongly that the time for embracing ignorance is long past. The church needs to be confronted with the truths that *make* captives free.

Bondage and ignorance are not the covenant of the saints of God. We should not suffer despair but strive to know truth as it is revealed by the Word of God, not man's interpretation. There is no other source by which we can know Christ intimately. It is his word alone, rightly divided, that renews the mind of the believer. In these pages, you'll see for yourselves the serious problems facing our Christian faith today. The knowledge gained will cause you to question and confront these issues for yourselves, in the light of God's unerring word. You'll see firsthand, as I have, the devastation that takes place when falsehoods are allowed to perpetuate in the church. Honestly, we're the ones who've allowed this to happen, because of our own ignorance of God's word. We've not challenged the darkness in the light of his glorious gospel for ourselves, but relegated it to the church. Often, we don't even know the truth(s) taught us in scripture, which have made us free. We categorically accept everything preached or taught us, without challenging a single thing. As a result, we find ourselves broken in our faith, unable to fix or even understand the problems plaguing us.

This book will address these problems and help us understand, with the aid of scripture, what we've allowed in our churches, which caused this condition to occur. Mankind is not your primary source for understanding all spiritual matters. God is your source. He certainly can and has used men and women of faith to convey spiritual truths, but ultimately you're the one responsible for what you believe. According to God's word, the buck stops with you. You're not to merely accept everything you hear without questioning anything. You're to challenge everything you hear according to the Word of God, to know what is true and what is not.

You've find that this book is loaded with scriptural references. The purposes for doing so are quite obvious. For out of the Bible flow all of the issues of life. I'll acquaint you with specific scriptures relating to the issues I'm discussing. You'll also learn that in order to understand the God of your salvation, you need to understand His word as it specifically relates to those issues, becoming dependent upon it for all areas of faith.

The Word of God is vital to everyone claiming to be born again. It's our supporting proof of everything we claim to believe. I leave nothing to chance or personal opinion. Rightly dividing the word of truth/scripture is something we must never take lightly. Seeking truth will always reward the seeker with joy unspeakable and full of glory. It is life to me and I hope to you as well.

I love scripture and enjoy getting to the real meat or intended meaning of it. The King James Version delivers that and so much more in my study of God's word. That is why I have chosen this particular version for most scriptural references you'll find in this book.

Those of you who picked this book may be experiencing one or all of the following:

1) Your hunger to understand the ways and deep things of God remains unsatisfied.
2) Your thirst for knowledge into the realm of the supernatural, in Christ, is like searching for a pool of clear cool refreshing

water to a desperately parched soul. You simply want and need more of it.

3) Your desire to possess for yourself all of God's promises has proved difficult, since you don't know what those promises actually entail.

Ephesians 3:19
"And to know the love of Christ, which passeth knowledge, that ye might be filled with all the fullness of God."

"That you might be filled with the fullness of God." What a glorious statement, but what does that really mean?

This means that when we're filled with all of the fullness of God, we have sufficiency in all things. Paul talks about being complete in all things, abounding in every good thing, never lacking, but possessing all things which pertain to life and godliness.

2 Peter 1:3
According as his divine power hath given unto us all things that pertain unto life and godliness, through the knowledge of him that hath called us to glory and virtue.

Here's the promise. When you drink of the water that Christ gives, you'll never thirst again spiritually.

The Samaritan women had come to Jacob's well, according to the Gospel of John, to fetch water. Jesus speaks to this woman and says, "Give me to drink." She responds by saying, "How is it that you, a Jew, would ask me, a Samaritan, to give you a drink of water?"

Please notice what the Lord tells her. It's awesome in its simplicity, but profoundly eternal. Out of left field, Jesus says to her, "If you knew the gift of God and who it is that asked you for a drink of water you would be asking *me* for living water."

Christ is not moved by what she says, but goes on to tell her, as recorded in John 4:13, that "whosoever drinketh of this water shall thirst again."

We know, from her response, that this woman didn't really grasp the significance of what Christ had said. She simply expressed what she knew: that the water from the well was the source of life for her and her people. Jesus, on the other hand, was taking this opportunity to minister to this woman about her (and our) spiritual condition. He used the natural thing to bring light and understanding about her supernatural or spiritual need, which she did not yet possess. The source for eternal life, "living water," could only come from him, the author of this life-altering, living water.

We know from scripture that there are four very important things concerning this living water.

1) Christ is the author, or gift-giver, of this life-giving water source.
2) Living water is immediately available to those who truly seek it.
3) It is free for the asking.
4) It is eternally sufficient for every need we'll ever have.

You see, this is precisely the place where most of God's people find themselves today. Like the woman at the well, they are in a continual place of thirsting. The children of God are drinking water that can never quench or satisfy the spiritual thirst of their souls. Off they go, to the well of water called the church, church programs, various ministry efforts, works, religious traditions, and so on. The result is always the same and quite predictable. They thirst and thirst and thirst again, ever returning to the well, but leaving unsatisfied.

A REAL-LIFE ILLUSTRATION

Have you ever experienced such a terrible thirst that without water, you felt you would surely die? I have. The experience is still fresh in my mind. I was hitchhiking across Colorado on foot many years ago and couldn't get anyone to pick me up. I literally walked across most of the state. During that trip, I had neither food nor water. I was famished and desperately thirsty, even to the point of death. There was no water to be found anywhere, but I finally did manage to find a small amount of water in a recess in the ground. The water was filthy dirty, with who knows what in it. But it was water and I was desperate. I got on my knees and drank every last bit of it.

In the realm of Christianity, you might say to yourself, "I'm dying of thirst spiritually," so you go to church for another glass of water, gulping it down. Afterward you discover that what you had received didn't quite satisfy you. You grab another glass, then another, but you just can't seem to satisfy your terrible thirst.

Like the woman at the well, the place where most Christians go for spiritual refreshing is unattainable in the flesh. What a horrible place to find oneself: spiritually thirsty and dry. But look at what the Lord says to us in verse 14 about the water that he alone gives:

John 4:14
But whosoever drinketh of the water that I shall give him shall never thirst; but the water that I shall give him shall be in him a well of water springing up into everlasting life.

Christ promises that the water he gives us will quench our spiritual thirst. He goes on to say that not only will it quench our thirst, but we will *never* thirst again. How marvelous is that? It will be inside of us, a well of water, continually springing up, even into everlasting life. A source that is never exhausted, or polluted; pure, sufficient for every need.

So, what's this everlasting life spoken of here? It's an intimate relationship with God the Father and Jesus Christ.

John 17:3
And this is life eternal, that they might know thee the only true God, and Jesus Christ, whom thou hast sent.

I find this promise to be absolutely amazing. That you, as an ordinary man or woman, might have complete intimacy with the true and living God.

He says that the water that he gives us to drink will spring up inside of us. This water brings us total satisfaction, which then keeps us so we will never thirst again or have a spiritual lack.

I wonder if you have that living water. The woman thought she had it in Jacob's well. Perhaps you too have a well you go to, but find no living water there. Daily you return to it, hoping to be satisfied one more time, but come away empty. Would you be honest enough to admit you really don't have the living water that Christ is talking about?

Those who have found this well of water springing up inside find a refreshing truth. Their thirst is *finally* quenched. Incredibly, there is no longer a lack in their lives. Seeking external gratification is no longer a necessity for them. They now serve instead of being served. The fountain from within overflows, and the lives of those around them are impacted in a positive way.

Let me make this observation. People go to the well to drink because they believe this source of water is blessed of God: Jacob's well. The church becomes their source, the place where the water is drawn. They do their drinking and return as often as thirst comes. It becomes a natural habit to expect refreshment from this source. You let the bucket down time and time again, day after day, week after week, and year after year, but nothing changes.

Jesus was clear: "If you drink of this water you will thirst again." It'll give you satisfaction, but be assured it's only a temporary fix. You'll be back!

What a great analogy. Wells of water bring life. This Samaritan woman understood Jacob's well provided life-giving properties. She even challenged Christ concerning its value to her, to her entire village, and even to him since he came because of his thirst. He, however, challenged her with *a greater spiritual truth*. It can be said that Jacob's well held a religious significance to the many who gathered there every day to draw water, though obviously they didn't understand that. All these folks knew was that it was from this well that life flowed to them and their community. They came out daily, or as the need arose, to draw the necessary water and be satisfied. The well had been provided by the patriarch for their use, and they treasured it.

Jesus simply took this opportunity to introduce her to a greater source of spiritual blessing, a well springing up on the inside unto eternal life, where the spiritual need(s) of the recipients would forever be quenched. He pointed to himself as the giver of this life-giving water, the well from which to draw, to those who would simply ask.

Here is another truth: Jacob's well speaks of a form of godliness that has no power in it. It can be further defined as anything that'll bring you temporary or fleshly satisfaction but is empty spiritually: the church you attend, the ministry you're involved in, programs designed by the organized church to help you in your quest to be holy. We call these things godly, but they deceive us. They never provide satisfaction. Our thirst is never satisfied. Worst of all, they take you further from the true source of living water. It keeps you from drinking from his well.

Only the *living water* which Christ gives springs or bursts forth into everlasting life. All other efforts are empty, vain attempts at satisfying the longing of our souls. You may think both of these things are the source of life, but don't be deceived. They are not.

The place we're to go to drink and eat is from him. Scripture says:

John 6:54-56
Whoso eateth my flesh, and drinketh my blood, hath eternal life; and I will raise him up at the last day.

> **For my flesh is meat indeed, and my blood is drink indeed.**

He that eateth my flesh, and drinketh my blood, dwelleth in me, and I in him.

Instead of rejoicing, the disciples took offense at what he said. Look at their response to his words. They were shocked and appalled by what he said. They thought he was talking to them about his physical body.

John 6:60
Many therefore of his disciples, when they had heard this, said, this is a hard saying; who can hear it?

I believe the time has come for those who are of like-minded faith to rise up, to have an ear to hear and an eye to see. There are people like you who have a longing to hear the small still voice, and the hunger and thirst for the living God.

Many are seeking and searching. They want to go beyond the brokenness of what they see around them to the new thing in Christ. They've witnessed the devastation caused by religion and desire something real and different. They don't want a different church, just a different type of relationship with Christ. The Christianity they see has become a failure to them. It doesn't lead them to living water. They see a parched and barren land, which is splintered and self-serving. They're tired of the status quo and want something that's spiritually real. The artificial and fleshly efforts of the church to know God no longer appeals to them. They long to eat the flesh and drink the blood of Christ. Theirs is a passion to *consume* the living God, coming into oneness both in intimacy and communion with him.

This "deal breaker" identified in the above scripture passage above separated those who truly wanted Jesus from those who merely followed him. We know that all of these disciples had witnessed the countless miracles of Christ and were among the large contingent of disciples sent out by Jesus to do ministry (Luke 10:1-9). Still, they were among those who departed when confronted with this impossibly hard saying.

Though a great many ceased following him, there were those who remained. They had just seen many of their friends leave and no doubt pondered leaving themselves. It was a very hard place for them, and Jesus knew it. But he had spoken hard things before, and now he wanted to expose what was in their hearts. Those remaining understood the gravity of what he had just said. Jesus then confronted them with another pointed question: "Will ye also go away?" (John 6:67).

I love Peter's response as recorded in John 6:68-69: "Then Simon Peter answered him, Lord, to whom shall we go? Thou hast the words of eternal life. And we believe and are sure that thou art that Christ, the son of the living God."

That was the deal breaker for them: "Thou hast the words of eternal life." At this point, they realized for themselves that regardless of who might leave, friends included, nothing would drag them away from their master. They were sold out to Christ at that moment (except for Judas, of course).

We too must stay committed to the master, though countless others retreat when hard sayings come. Our contract with religion and the ways of the world must be broken, and a new contract or covenant made with Christ.

These words must be applied to each of us if we're to experience this eternal life.

John 6:54-56
Whoso eateth my flesh, and drinketh my blood, hath eternal life.

The word says that whosoever eats my flesh and drinks my blood has *eternal life*. There is little doubt that this was a difficult saying, but Christ wanted them to work through the hardness of it so they might drink in the sweet truth he wanted them to understand. Make no mistake: he loved every last one of these disciples. He didn't want any of them to leave. He wasn't trying to weed out the undesirables.

But if they were to remain as his disciples, they needed to know why it was that they were staying and what the cost of staying would be.

The depth of a disciple's commitment to their master was and still is measured by the truths they're willing to accept. True disciples may falter from time to time, but in the end their commitment to stay far outweighs the ease of leaving because of a difficult word.

Remember what Christ said to the woman at the well? If you knew the gift of God, if you knew the gift that God desires to give to you, a well of water springing up in you unto everlasting life (John 4:6).

John 4:15 records her reply: "The woman saith unto him, Sir, give me this water, that I thirst not."

That, my friend, is my heartfelt prayer for you. That by the time you've finished reading this book, you'll no longer be the same; that in you, Christianity will not be broken. When the words you've read are no longer just words, but have become life in you.

And that new life, his life, will bring you out from under the cloak of the fractured and splintered Christianity you've grown accustomed to and allow you to walk in the finished work of the atonement of Jesus Christ.

CHAPTER 1
HOW IS CHRISTIANITY BROKEN?

Ask any Christian about the concept of a broken Christianity, and you'll get some angry responses and denials. Strangely, those outside of the realm of the church couldn't agree more with the title of this book.

I am convinced the church, as a whole, likes to see itself through rose-colored glasses. They see themselves as holy and undefiled; without flaws or failures; needing nothing. In fact, Christians are steadfastly convinced that they are prime examples of righteousness to the world in which they live, an example of what godly living is all about.

On the other hand, people outside of the church have a more realistic view of what they see in Christianity. They see hypocrisy everywhere, both in the churches and the people who attend. They see a church that is way past its usefulness, dying a slow, unhappy death. Its little wonder they avoid it at all cost.

Unbelievers are undoubtedly perplexed when they hear proclamations by Christians of loving God and mankind. Yet there is nothing for them to see which display it. "Where's the power of the God they serve?" they wonder.

Christians don't shake the earth as they once did. Certainly not like Paul and his contemporaries. Listen to what he has to say about his faith:

Romans 1:16
For I am not ashamed of the gospel of Christ: for it is the power of God unto salvation to everyone that believeth; to the Jew first, and also to the Greek.

What about you, Christian? Do you believe the church of today is a broken institution, or the same victorious church of days gone by? How is the power of God working in the lives of your friends—in you? Do you see your faith and the faith of your friends as that of a strong athletic runner, dashing with all strength toward the finish line, or do you see them running it as men lame and crippled? Perhaps we are ashamed of the true gospel of Christ.

Like most folks, I too would like to see a vibrant church, filled with men and women of faith, people who aren't ashamed of the gospel of Christ. But things are going to have to change if that's ever to happen again.

When I say to you that Christianity is broken, what am I implying? After all, this is a very strong statement to make. Truth can be a hard pill to swallow, but it can be sweet tasting to those longing for it. Honestly, it grieves me terribly to see Christianity in the mess that it's in today. Who's at fault; who should we blame?

Have you wondered what the word broken really means or implies?

Let's start with a definition. "Broken" implies any of these things:

1) That something isn't working
2) That broken means defeated
3) That it's been shattered or fractured
4) That it's something that is out of order

Whenever you see an "out of order" sign on a candy or pop machine, what do you usually do? You simply walk by, unwilling to invest anything in it because you'll end up losing your money. The sign says so!

The machine no longer functions as it was meant to. You also know from experience that it's silly to put money into a machine that doesn't work, because you'll lose it.

Haven't you ever had those same thoughts when it comes to your faith? You struggle with thoughts of despair, hopelessness, and frustration as you've endeavored to faithfully walk in Christianity; even when you thought it wasn't really working for you. Others, like you, did everything that they knew to do. They gave generously. They prayed, fasted, and diligently sought the face of the Lord, only to remain troubled and overwhelmed by the things which were coming against them, seemingly never being able to rise above them.

There was always a token encouragement from those watching you struggle. They applauded your efforts and cheered you on with encouraging words like, "Hang in there, you can do it. Be strong. Have faith. Lean on the Lord," and so on. But you didn't feel that any of that helped. Your feelings were wrapped around your failures, disappointments, and self-imposed unworthiness. While you experienced broken and dysfunctional relationships, the encouragement of well-meaning church members provided little comfort. Well, you are not alone. This is the same heart cry of many children of God.

Multitudes of Christians are engulfed in destructive habits that imprison the weak. They remain undelivered. The youth of today struggle, trying to see the bigger spiritual picture, but it's not clear to them. In fact, it's no less confusing to those who're trying to explain the picture to them. Confusion abounds. The blind are leading the blind.

Multitudes are drinking water from wells that are not springing up into everlasting life. Their wells are stagnant, filled with death. But they continue to come back to the same old well. They feel trapped and helpless, desiring water that'll quench their spiritual thirst, but find none. They reason that drinking water from the well of Christianity, even in its broken state, is better than dying of thirst. So it continues.

There are a great many people who have heard about the well that springs up into everlasting life, but they don't know how to acquire it. It sounds wonderful but completely unattainable to them, like the mythical fountain of youth. It's a well springing up somewhere for someone, but it's certainly not springing up inside them. Its location appears to be a tightly guarded secret.

Remarkably, the truth that promises to make you free is the same truth that few in the church want to hear. They like the status quo, the "let's not rock the boat" mentality.

The "too good to be true" Good News appears too good to be a reality in the lives of those actually needing it. The perfect law of liberty we're commanded to walk in then becomes a law of bondage, because we don't understand it.

James 1:25 says, "But whoso looketh into the perfect law of liberty, and continueth therein, he being not a forgetful hearer, but a doer of the work, this man shall be blessed in his deed."

How can this be when we claim to have such a great salvation and Messiah? For what purpose and what function has this "so great salvation" then come to us?

What makes Christianity real is that it separates us from every other religion or denomination on the earth. It's your intimate relationship with the true and living God, which brings your transformation.

Transformation in the eyes of God is your intimate relationship with him that takes place when you surrender yourself completely for the sake of intimacy. The change is a radical one, where "old things are passed away, and behold, all things become new." It's a marriage made in heaven with the Lord of glory.

2 Corinthians 5:17
Therefore if any man be in Christ, he is a new creature: old things are passed away; behold, all things are become new.

Any man that is found in Christ is a new creature, never having existed before; where all things have literally passed away and behold, *all things have become new*.

Ephesians 2:2-6
Wherein in time past ye walked according to the course of this world, according to the prince of the power of the air, the spirit that now worketh in the children of disobedience: Among whom also we all had our conversation in times past in the lusts of our flesh, fulfilling the desires of the flesh and of the mind; and were by nature the children of wrath, even as others.
But God, who is rich in mercy, for his great love wherewith he loved us, even when we were dead in sins, hath quickened us together with Christ (by grace ye are saved); and hath raised us up together, and made us sit together in heavenly places in Christ Jesus.

THE SIMPLICITY OF SALVATION IS FOUND IN THIS SINGLE VERSE:

John 3:16
For God so loved the world, that he gave his only begotten son, that whosoever believeth in him should not perish, but have everlasting life.

This scripture tells us the wonderful things afforded the person who believes in the resurrected Christ. But there are some things that it does not say directly, though they are implied. For one, it does not emphasize that salvation is our way of escaping an eternity in hell, though that is true. It also does not emphasize that salvation provides forgiveness of sins, though forgiveness of our sins is included.

The real importance of what this scripture is saying is simple. God so loved the world, that he gave his only begotten son, that whosoever shall believe in him shall not perish but have *everlasting life*. Christ came to give the special gift of *everlasting life* to those who believed in him. Therein is the focus and primary implied truth of the gospel as stated by this simple scripture.

You might not think that's so important to understand, but it is the very foundation of Christianity. *Jesus came to give us everlasting life.* Now that's life worth living for.

Will you be delivered from the depths of hell if you are born again? Absolutely you will! Will your sins be forgiven if you are born again? Absolutely they are!

Though these are important truths to enjoy because of salvation, neither of these was his primary motivation or reason for coming to this earth. He had a higher purpose in mind: *everlasting life*, with him and the Father.

I acknowledge that Christ died for our sins, and what a blessing that is. But redeeming us from sin was just a small part of his coming. We've unfortunately made forgiveness of sins the larger part; emphasizing its great role in the salvation experience. Little do we know how great an injustice we've done to new believers. We've minimized the value of the very greatest gift, *everlasting life,* to them, relegating it as a future bonus benefit that'll be revealed for all believers at our death: a place in heaven.

I shall always be thankful that my sins, which were scarlet, have been made white as snow by his sacrifice, and that my sins and yours are now cast as far from us and him as the east is from the west, into the sea of forgetfulness—forever. But let me focus all my remaining days on the real benefit of his coming, that according to the Word of God, he might usher in *everlasting life* for us, here. Most Christians are never taught that the gift of everlasting life is a present-day necessity, not some future event.

Our sins obviously needed to be forgiven, but not for the reasons you have been taught. Christ knew that sin separated us from him and everlasting life. Sin also stood in the way of a right relationship with God, and he could not bear this separation. Mankind had been made in the image of God. It was his choice to do so, because he wanted and longed to fellowship, have *everlasting life*, with his creation.

Sin was the barrier between us and God. Christ paid the price for your sin through his atonement. This destroyed the sin barrier forever. We were fully restored in fellowship with the Father because of this thing called *everlasting life*, his gift to anyone who accepted Christ in faith.

I'm so thankful to the Father and Jesus his son for this restoration and this promised gift.

Never forget, friends, the real purpose of salvation is and always will be *everlasting life*.

CHAPTER 2
WHAT IS ETERNAL LIFE?

Without a doubt, understanding eternal life, as it is clearly defined in scripture and described in this book, should be the church's primary mission here on the earth. We, you and I, and others like us are that church, the collective body of believers, not organized religion or a specific denomination.

When we understand this life-giving principle for ourselves, we can then instruct others in this vital element of salvation. It is God's chosen method for drawing all men unto himself, through intimacy.

HERE IS WHAT ORGANIZED RELIGION TEACHES US ABOUT ETERNAL LIFE:

1) That eternal life is the forgiveness of sins.
2) That eternal life means your name is written in the Lamb's Book of Life.
3) That eternal life means living forever in heaven with God.
4) That eternal life means you'll escape the fires of hell.

Most children of God believe that everlasting life is a future or end time event, in a spiritual realm yet to be revealed.

The correct answer to the question, "What is everlasting life?" is that it's a gift of God for you, right here, right now. It's a present tense possession.

SEE FOR YOURSELVES IN THIS SCRIPTURE:

John 3:36
He that believeth on the son hath everlasting life: and he that believeth not the son shall not see life; but the wrath of God abideth on him.

PLEASE READ IT ONCE AGAIN:

"He that believeth on the son *hath* [present tense: or "now has"] everlasting life."

You receive everlasting life at the very instant you become born again. Accepting Christ into your life merely scratches the spiritual surface of everything we receive as joint heirs with him. This is a difficult thing for 99 percent of all Christians to grasp. Most think that salvation is forgiveness of sins only, believing it doesn't get any better than this. That is what they've been taught. Well, let me tell you something: they're wrong. That's like saying the Pearly Gates is all that you'll find in heaven. Obviously, that's silly. Once you've entered through these gates of pearl, there are glories that are so magnificent that man simply cannot fathom them. It'll take countless ages, eternity in fact, to grasp the entirety of what God has prepared for them that love him. The Apostle Paul was blown away by what he heard and saw while transported to the third heaven (John 12:2-4).

People who are not properly instructed by mature men and women of faith will always see themselves as sinners saved by grace, never grasping the fullness of all Christ has done and given. It's impossible for you to go any further than what you learn.

Most Christians believe that everlasting life is simply living forever, which is a partial truth. But they never question anyone (or search God's word) concerning the greater truth as it's being revealed here. So they can only relate to John 3:16 in the very simplest of terms.

HERE'S THE TRUTH:

Everyone lives forever! There isn't one person who'll ever live on this earth who doesn't eventually die. Though they're separated from their physical bodies in death, the spirit body and soul are still quite alive. Your existence has merely been changed to a different realm, known as eternity. The place called eternity is just as vivid and real to them, though we cannot see it or them with our mortal eyes. The Word of God says so.

There is no such thing as life ending when your physical body dies. Some say that death is the final chapter, but that is absolutely false. In reality, it's only the beginning. We live a short mortal life here on earth, but an eternal life that never ends once we've died our natural death. Everybody lives forever somewhere, heaven or hell, and they will continue to do so because God has established it by his word. And his word never fails.

LET ME BRING YOU BACK TO THIS SCRIPTURE:

John 3:36
He that believeth on the son hath everlasting life.

Remember, this only applies to those who are born again, no one else. Neither does this scripture talk about some future event. As stated, it's specific to the present condition of the born-again believer.

If I were to paraphrase it for simplicity sake, I would simply tell you that you receive everlasting life immediately upon your acceptance of Jesus Christ. Anyone who has ever taken English in school understands that this is spoken in the present tense, which applies to your human life right now: "He that believeth on the son *hath* everlasting life."

HERE ARE OTHER HELPFUL VERSES:

John 5:24
Verily, verily, I say unto you, he that heareth my word, and believeth on him that sent me, hath everlasting life, and shall not come into condemnation; but is passed from death unto life.

John 6:47
Verily, verily ["truly, truly": my words], **I say unto you, he that believeth on me hath everlasting life.**

You should have no confusion about an event in the future. It is what it says.

I have frequently noticed how many Christians get confused over the simplest things. They see their lives as a living reality, but they don't understand or see the spirit realm as a greater reality, one which is both active and alive, already established, though unseen.

This next scripture gives you a window from which to view truth concerning everlasting life. Thank goodness everlasting life is a present tense reality. It's the passing from spiritual death into spiritual life. There is no condemnation in this place, only freedom from it, to them that believe.

Everlasting life is an intimate relationship with God that doesn't have to wait to be enjoyed. How glorious for everyone seeking to know God in a more personal way.

John 17:2-3
As thou hast given him power over all flesh, that he should give eternal life to as many as thou hast given him.
And this is life eternal, that they might know thee the only true God, and Jesus Christ, whom thou hast sent.
Do you realize just how powerful and wonderful this statement is? Everlasting life is in our knowing, intimately, the only true God and Jesus Christ, who was sent. It's hard to fathom how completely contrary this is to the denominational view of eternal life. We know

that Christians aren't properly instructed in the biblical truths of God's word. This results in wholesale confusion on their part, coupled with the misinterpretation of these and other scriptural passages. As a result, most folks flounder when it comes to the difficult issues of faith. Like the disciples mentioned earlier, we'll abandon the very place Christ wants us to remain because of a hard teaching. People who are firmly grounded will remain, even though the teaching is hard, but many will leave.

A TIP FOR SPIRITUAL HEALTH:

Remember, you can only be instructed to the level or degree of the spiritual insight of the person doing the teaching or preaching. If they don't understand or properly discern scripture, as God intends, it only stands to reason that it will be nearly impossible for you to understand it either. The natural thing for most Christians is to simply believe everything they're told, without questioning anything. "He's the pastor, so he must know what he's talking about," they say. Are you willing to stake your spiritual well-being on that kind of rationale? Not me. I check out everything, regardless of who preaches it. I want to make sure the things they preach line up with scripture. If not, I ask questions.

It is very difficult for you to gain ground in your walk with Christ in this kind of environment, unless you do your own independent study. This is the primary reason I instruct people to challenge everything they hear. They need to read and study scripture for themselves, regardless of who their preacher is or who their teachers are. If you'll plant the seed of faith into your study of God's word, a harvest of clarity and understanding will surely come. It is the promise of God for sowing and reaping. Remember, the Holy Spirit is your guide into all truth. He will not disappoint those who truly long to know the deep things of God. On the other hand, if you don't do this, you'll be constantly frustrated, never getting a real grasp of who God is inside of you. Spiritual principles, which should be simple to understand, will seem impossible to understand. Holding all teachers and preachers accountable for the words they proclaim is our right and responsibility. Your spiritual health depends on it.

Remember, these statements are not word gymnastics to confuse you; they're the Word of God, which need to be rightly divided to understand their true meaning.

Some of God's people will scream at such things, thinking I've lost my mind. How many of God's people do you think would be disappointed at hearing this? Their response might be something like, "You mean to tell me that is all eternal life is: knowing God?" Yes indeed!

"Well, I *know* God," they'll exclaim. In fact, most people who proclaim to be born-again Christians and who attend church regularly will emphatically claim that they know God and how God works. If that is so, then why is there such confusion and frustration in the body of Christ today? Why is there a greater emphasis placed on programs and entertainment than knowing the Word of God in fullness? Many say that the church needs to draw people, and programs and entertainment are effective. I'll agree that events and other programs do draw people, but very seldom is anyone changed by them. Only the Word of God changes the sinful heart of man. If you bring them with entertainment, you'll always need to do something more spectacular the next time to bring them back.

Here's something for you to grasp:
Actually, the word "know" in John 17:3 isn't talking about an intellectual knowledge at all. It's not talking about knowing how the church works or how a certain denomination functions, rather, it describes "intimacy" with God. The word "know" or "knew" is the same word used in the Word of God to describe the most intimate relationship that men and women can have personally. Read below.

Genesis 4:1
And Adam knew Eve his wife; and she conceived, and bare Cain, and said, I have gotten a man from the Lord.

Genesis 4:25
And Adam knew his wife again; and she bare a son, and called his name Seth: for God, said she, hath appointed me another seed instead of Abel, whom Cain slew.

This is a personal, loving intimacy with one another as joined in union through marriage. Eternal life is being defined and described by the Lord Jesus Christ as intimacy with God and himself.

Keep in mind that the one describing *eternal life* is actually the same author of this *eternal life*. Jesus never misspeaks. He clearly understands what he says and to whom it's being said. But as usual, we like to mix our human knowledge and intellect with spiritual truths, coming up with meanings that are convoluted, or mixed up entirely. We'll claim, "This is what Jesus really means." If Christ really meant it any other way, he would have said it another way. He longs to have his children understand precisely what he means. It doesn't benefit you or the Kingdom of God if you're confused.

Hebrews 5:9
And being made perfect, he became the author of eternal salvation unto all them that obey him.

This is intimate relationship with God, or intimacy in its purest form.

John 3:16
For God so loved the world, that he gave his only begotten son, that whosoever believeth in him should not perish, but have [intimacy with God].

We can interject any of the following phrases into John 3:16, and the meaning will remain unchanged:

But have a personal relationship . . .
But have an intimate relationship . . .
But have a close relationship . . .
But have life abundantly . . .

But have complete communion . . .
But have unity . . . with God and his son, the Lord Jesus Christ.

Here's something to let sink into your spirit. The reason that the Lord Jesus Christ came to this earth was to bring you into intimate relationship with God and himself. Period! But this is not the message that most of us have heard from the pulpit. Their message is one of fear and condemnation: "Repent ye sinners, or else." God is angry because of your sin. Preachers tell their congregations that fear and condemnation is the Good News spoken of in scripture.

I ask you honestly: Do you really sense the love of Christ and the Father being conveyed from this kind of message? It doesn't sound like Good News to me, nor am I sure to anyone else confronted in this manner. But it's the common denominator among many churches today.

Few churches carry the message of the unconditional love of God to those dying in their sin. Generally, there's nothing about intimacy or everlasting life, as described in this book. We've only been taught to come to Christ when we have specific needs. Intimacy is seldom, if ever, encouraged, generally because the pastors or teachers know nothing about intimacy themselves. As a result, our only interaction with Christ or God the Father is when we feel a pressing need or have a problem that needs fixing. Desperation sets in, and we plead for him to come down and do something for us.

The emphasis is only on the things we feel are most needed to keep our lives comfortable, instead of the relationship that brings all things. You need a different relationship than the one you have right now, one that is close, personal, and intimate with God and the Lord Jesus Christ.

It would be a sad marriage if our partner were only interested in what satisfied his or her own needs. "What's in this relationship for me?" they'd ask. I see it everywhere in the churches I visit. These marriages seldom last long, as you can imagine. It doesn't take a rocket scientist to figure out where the problem is.

The church experience leaves the average Christian tenuous at best. Most have a strong reluctance to approach God on any level, believing that doing so will result in yet another trial or test. For them, God is quick to judge and remains angry with us because of our sins. This mischaracterizes what the Bible clearly says: God is tender, loving, and compassionate to his children, which is the real Good News of the Gospel. It's not about turning from the wrath of God. It never was. Satan has been successful in using the false message of God's wrath. Pastors, teachers, and well-meaning people have deceived multitudes, though in ignorance. It's clear that Satan has been very successful in this effort. Wouldn't you agree?

Here are some terrible misconceptions and untruths you'll readily identify with concerning the things being taught today.

1) That it's about turning from your wicked ways quickly and repenting, so you'll escape the immediate repercussions from God because of the sins you commit.
2) That eternal destruction waits for you and everyone like you, if you don't receive Jesus Christ, or become born again.
3) That it's about the debt you owe because of what Christ has done and how one day you'll give an account to him for your misdeeds, if you don't act right now.

The message of peace that's conveyed in scripture, being rightly divided, is nothing like these things. The Word of God talks of love, forgiveness, restoration, oneness with God and his son, Jesus Christ. God is not a hate-monger. He loves his creation and longs to have us back in his sheepfold, where he can lovingly tend to all of our needs. He even loved us while we were yet in sin. To prove the point, he sent his son.

1 John 4:7-10
Beloved, let us love one another: for love is of God; and everyone that loveth is born of God, and knoweth God.
He that loveth not knoweth not God; for God is love.

In this was manifested the love of God toward us, because that God sent his only begotten son into the world, that we might live through him.
Herein is love, not that we loved God, but that he loved us, and sent his son to be the propitiation for our sins.

He came that we might have everlasting life and that more abundantly. If Christ came to give us everlasting life, and life abundant, why do you suppose the message we hear creates such fear among the people? Why would the church want to drive sinners to Christ instead of leading them to him?

Have you ever noticed how fear is a great motivator? It'll prompt people to the altar, but generally it'll never last for the majority of them. It's because it's not a life-changing event for them. There's no love in what they hear, only condemnation if they don't respond. After a brief experience in the church setting, it's little wonder why people leave, seldom returning. Those who stay usually end up hopping from church to church, looking for a gentler God. Who wants to hear the same old condemnation message again and again?

All of us have had similar experiences. Some have been elevated to positions of leadership only to continue the cycle with those beneath them, believing they too are telling the true gospel. We mirror what we've been taught, so the message never has an opportunity to change. Then we're confounded when people leave the church.

Here's a good question for you:
Why do people who have been to the altar so many times in their lives never seem to encounter a true life-changing experience with God?

I believe one of the primary reasons is their true motive. It certainly isn't to enter into a personal, intimate relationship with Christ, but merely to escape something unpleasant. Fear and condemnation drive them to the altar. Coming, they're comforted with the notion that their need will be met. But once the service is over, off they go until the next time. Their lives aren't changed. It's back to living the same old way.

You honestly have heartfelt desire to see them change and to experience oneness with Christ, but the methods we use are wrong. The penitent person wasn't expecting anything beyond token forgiveness from God, because they weren't taught something greater was available. Thus, they never encounter this loving God of the Bible who wants nothing more than to surrender himself totally to his children in oneness through everlasting life. For them, God is not their friend; not the air they breathe, not the food they eat, nor the water they drink. The thought of such things is too difficult for them to grasp.

HERE'S A CONSISTENT PROBLEM IN THE BODY OF CHRIST:

Most of God's children don't have the proper motivation or desire to enter into a personal, intimate relationship with God. They've not been taught that the reason Christ came to this earth was to reestablish that relationship.

When the motive is to possess or gain a personal, intimate relationship with God, then the encounter becomes life changing for that individual.

The message that the early church taught was one of a personal and intimate relationship with God. It was about a quality of life that was vastly different from what they'd experienced in the past through religion. This new faith identified with God on a level of personal intimacy, not based on the sacrifices they'd previously made to appease an angry God. It was through intimacy that the gifts of the spirit would now operate and the fruits of the spirit would flow. From intimacy with God, all things pertaining to life and godliness would be made manifest to them in fullness.

When fear is gone, love remains.

CHAPTER 3
PERFECT LOVE CASTS OUT ALL FEAR

1 John 4:17-18
Herein is our love made perfect, that we may have boldness in the day of judgment: because as he is, so are we in this world. There is no fear in love; but perfect love casteth out fear: because fear hath torment. He that feared is not made perfect in love.

Have you ever considered what this scripture, "but perfect love cast out all fear," is actually telling you?

This scripture is generally in direct confrontation to the way that most of God's children today live their lives.

I wonder how many Christians would actually admit that they serve God out of fear.

1) They remain in constant fear of losing their salvation.
2) They serve God out of the fear of doing something wrong or making wrong choices.
3) They serve God out of the irrational fear of being punished, resulting in the withdrawal of his benefits and goodness toward them.

Fear to them becomes the dominant force in their lives. And they are most miserable because of it. Scripture tells you that this type of fear brings great torment, where the fear of God is quite literal. In this place, there is no reverence for a God who you believe is constantly seeking ways to punish you for your misdeeds.

The Word of God emphatically tells us that the reason this torment is present is because we've not been made perfect in love. How simple is this principal, yet profound?

Even Christians who have read this scripture countless times still don't understand what it's really saying. Fear hath torment; plain and simple. This torment brings great pain in your relationship with God (or in any relationship, for that matter).

ILLUSTRATION

We've all seen bad relationships between men and women, where fear causes one of them to stay in the relationship, though it causes them great torment and suffering.

One of the primary reasons that you don't have an intimate relationship with God is because you don't have a clear understanding of how much God really loves you—in spite of your failures and sin. Your love is not perfect toward God because it's motivated by a negative attitude: the fear of God. Love is the motivation for God. It should be motivation enough for you too.

Religions around the world operate the same. They tell you that you can't do this and you can't do that, or judgment will fall. This sounds familiar, doesn't it? I find it interesting that Christianity functions like every other religion on earth, when God tells us we're to be separate, a peculiar people.

In the Bible, we see what religion does to people. Beyond the scope of God's mandated laws, the Pharisees and Sadducees rode roughshod over their flocks by minutely dictating how the Jews were to act under any given circumstance. Their religion was full of bondage, not of love. They demanded obedience from the Jews and could inflict as much misery upon an individual as they liked. They told you how unworthy you were, while exalting their perceived perfection.

Luke 18:10-11 says, "Two men went up into the temple to pray; the one a Pharisee, and the other a publican. The Pharisee stood and prayed thus with himself, God, I thank thee, that I am not as other men are, extortioners, unjust, adulterers, or even as this publican."

Jesus condemned them for this and other things, calling them hypocrites and white-washed sepulchers, full of dead man's bones and of all uncleanness (Matthew 23.27). That's why they hated Jesus and sought ways to destroy him.

HERE IS MAN'S VIEW OF RELIGION:

1) Religion is about God's rejection of mankind.
2) Religion is criticism of how you live your life.
3) Religion is about what you must do, by performance, to please Almighty God.
4) Religion is about how you must walk in the presence of God, according to the mandates of the church.

If you're serving God under these conditions, it's no wonder that you don't enjoy living for him. You find no pleasure in reading, studying, or meditating on the Word of God, because to know more about him only brings more anxiety and condemnation. You tell yourself, "What I don't know can't hurt me."

If you're doing things to please God, so he'll be pleased and happy with you, scripture says you're tormented! Anytime you use negative measures to try and bring about positive results, you'll always end up with results that are flawed.

When Christ came to this earth, he came to give you everlasting life.

John 3:16
For God so loved the world, that he gave his only begotten son, that whosoever believeth in him should not perish, but have everlasting life.

LET ME SHOW YOU THE TRUTHS OF THESE SCRIPTURES:

John 3:36
He that believeth on the son hath everlasting life: and he that believeth not the son shall not see life; but the wrath of God abideth on him.

John 4:14
But whosoever drinketh of the water that I shall give him shall never thirst; but the water that I shall give him shall be in him a well of water springing up into everlasting life.

John 5:24
Verily, verily, I say unto you, he that heareth my word, and believeth on him that sent me, hath everlasting life, and shall not come into condemnation; but is passed from death unto life.

John 6:40
And this is the will of him that sent me, that everyone which seeth the son, and believeth on him, may have everlasting life: and I will raise him up at the last day.

You are correct: Our sins do need to be forgiven, because sin separates us from God. It's a barrier that needed to be broken down first, which Christ did at Calvary. No longer would hell threaten us or be reserved for us because of our unbelief. What a great assurance for the child of God. These are wonderful truths, but those are not the reasons that God gave humanity his son. Jesus came to give the world the real Good News of the gospel. The life that the children of Israel (and, for that matter, the rest of us) had before Christ was about to change dramatically and forever. Jesus came to pour out his mercy and grace upon all humanity, so that we might have eternal life and an intimate relationship with him.

God loved us so much that he sent his only begotten son, that you and I could experience a personal and intimate relationship with him and his son. This is the real motivation of salvation, the reason for his coming. There is no fear in this place and certainly no torment. Being rejected by God isn't possible now because of the atonement of Christ. He has accepted us fully in the beloved—Jesus. If you're in Christ, through the salvation experience, then the Father sees only his son when he looks at you, and he is pleased and fully satisfied. The sin issue has been resolved completely and forever; put aside, in fact, so that there is no longer anything that can hinder intimacy with him and his son, Jesus. This intimacy isn't for some future event, but to be enjoyed in this present life now and then on into everlasting life.

How does this occur? Because love is made perfect in Christ! Everything in the Word of God springs forth because of relationship, intimacy, and personal communion with God. If anything, God hates being separated from his creations. They were created for him to enjoy as much as we were created to enjoy him. Now, that's *love*! Isn't that what a marriage is all about? Think about that for a while. True love causes you to despise anything that separates you from that union, that oneness with your chosen mate. God hath chosen us, and we have chosen him: love.

When fear is your motivation, you are tormented, which is a result of not comprehending this next scripture:

Ephesians 3:17-20
That Christ may dwell in your hearts by faith; that ye, being rooted and grounded in love, may be able to comprehend with all saints what is the breadth, and length, and depth, and height; and to know the love of Christ, which passeth knowledge, that ye might be filled with all the fullness of God.

Now unto him that is able to do exceeding abundantly above all that we ask or think, according to the power that worketh in us.

Eternal life is manifested to God's children.

Chapter 4

Eternal Life Manifested

In the last three chapters, I explained the purpose of salvation, why God the Father gave his son, and the real reason for coming to earth in the first place. We learned that it was necessary to reestablish intimacy with Almighty God and that everything pertaining to life and godliness springs forth from this intimacy.

Countless Christians feel frustrated in their walk with Christ. They have little assurance that what they're doing is right in the eyes of God. They do what seems right for them to do, but they never discover the real truth about these efforts, which God calls dead works.

Examples of dead works:

1) Works by human effort or good deeds
2) Works by making the right choices as dictated by social conscience
3) Works by feeding and clothing the poor in their respective communities
4) Works of obedience by personal strivings
5) Works by human faith

Real life only comes through the Lord Jesus Christ. The true abundant life can only be achieved through intimacy with God. Otherwise, all of our efforts are in vain.

HERE'S SOMETHING YOU SHOULD KNOW:

A great number of people who've had their sins forgiven do not have an intimate relationship with Jesus Christ or God. Because intimacy is not in place, they experience very little joy in their lives and lack understanding concerning the ways of God. This ultimately results in no real spiritual fruit being produced, which should be the hallmark of our lives in Christ, as described in scripture. Since no real revelation is received, they have neither freedom nor liberty in the beloved. They see the whole experience as unfulfilling, but certainly demanding and taxing.

Within their salvation experience, Christians sense an obligation to God, but they aren't sure how to fulfill it. Inadequate preaching or instruction brings frustration to their experience because they feel they're getting mixed messages. They mistake service to God for intimacy; thinking that their good intentions and efforts are what God expects and what will ultimately please him.

An effective example in scripture concerning this very issue is what I call "Mary and Martha—an intimacy illustration":

Luke 10:38-42 (Amplified Version)
Now while they were on their way, it occurred that Jesus entered a certain village, and a woman named Martha received and welcomed Him into her house.
And she had a sister named Mary, who seated herself at the Lord's feet and was listening to His teaching.
But Martha [overly occupied and too busy] was distracted with much serving; and she came up to Him and said, Lord, is it nothing to you that my sister has left me to serve alone? Tell her then to help me [to lend a hand and do her part along with me]!
But the Lord replied to her by saying, Martha, Martha, you are anxious and troubled about many things;
There is need of only one or but a few things. Mary has chosen the good portion [that which is to her advantage], which shall not be taken away from her.

How many people do you know who fit this category? An awful lot, I'm guessing. They serve God out of obedience and obligation, but there's no intimate, personal, or close communion with him. They have other relationships and purported intimacy with other church members, but this never brings long-term satisfaction either. To most, the excitement of serving Christ has long worn off. The demands on them now seem to get greater, and the requirements for maintaining their salvation seem never ending. They're both exhausted and frustrated. After a while, they merely go through the motions, saying, "I'm just suffering to please Jesus." So it seems, but it's not God's plan for their lives.

Things obviously need to be done in a church setting. It takes tremendous effort and hard work to run churches, and there are so precious few doing all the work. It doesn't seem fair, does it? But please reread verse 42 again, and you'll see that Christ immediately saw the difference between Mary and her sister. He loved Martha just as much as Mary, but only one of them sought spiritual intimacy with him: Mary. While Martha was troubled with other things (if you will, the affairs of the church), she found herself frustrated and bitter. She couldn't enjoy what Mary enjoyed, because she saw herself in the same light that most of God's children see themselves today; there's simply too much to do and so little time to get it all done. They think to themselves, "Somebody has to do the work, and I don't see anyone else coming forward to help out. Hopefully, God will be pleased with my efforts."

Mary, on the other hand, couldn't get enough of Jesus's presence. She wanted him above all else: his teachings, presence, fellowship, and ministry. It must have seemed to her that there was so much she needed to absorb and too little time to get it done. Mary wasn't about to miss a thing, so she stuck close to Jesus. Why waste time with natural food, when you can eat from the table of the master? This supernatural food was her delight: "to eat his flesh and drink his blood." There would always be time for the other things, the necessities of life, but the better thing is always intimacy. She chose that portion, and Christ said it wouldn't be denied her.

If you haven't noticed, Christianity is at a critical crossroads today. Look around. It's easy to see. The churches are disintegrating before our very eyes because of this nonsense. Emotions run deep, but real joy is hard to find. They love God, but not through intimacy. They serve the church as slaves do their masters, being told that God is pleased with their much suffering and hard work. They love God through their works, not faith and certainly not intimacy.

When was the last time you were told just how much God longs to have intimacy with his children—*you*? That through intimacy, God would reveal to his precious children all of the mysteries of himself and what salvation through his son means. He wants joy to be as bountiful in your life as it is in his. Something terrible is missing: the truth!

God's children are like the wind-up dolls that you find at Wal-Mart. Simply wind them up, point them in the direction of service that fits their church's need, and off they go to do the "good things" you what them to do. To help them in their efforts, we perpetuate the untruths of how pleased God is. So struggle on, brothers and sisters, your reward is just waiting for you, way down the suffering road. Perhaps you can identify with this. Most children of God can. From the altar, they're programmed to be a part of the organized church structure, or denomination, instead of toward intimacy with God. The Christian life you see today is not the way that Christian life was *ever* meant to be, nor was it that way in the early church.

What is intimacy? Isn't it a communion relationship with a person that truly loves you and you love them in return? *Intimacy is always two sided, never one sided.* When you witness for yourself what true love is, you'll find great pleasure in having that love fully encompass you. You'll know that there is oneness in this love and know it's real. This perfect love does not hinder you in the least, but makes you freer than you've ever been in your mortal life.

There are four parts of the salvation experience, documented in scripture, which make you free. Most are aware that salvation brings with it the forgiveness of sins, but very few know (or were taught) that there are actually four parts to salvation.

HERE ARE THE FOUR PARTS:

1) *Part 1:* you know that you have been completely forgiven of all sin.
2) *Part 2:* you know that you have been completely healed, free from any disease.
3) *Part 3:* you know that you have been delivered in every possible area.
4) *Part 4:* you know that you have been made prosperous, financially prosperous.

All of these gifts were given to you *immediately*, when you received Christ as Savior and Lord, or what is commonly called being *born again*. Please note that there is no lag time with any of these gifts. Because of God's great love of humankind, in that he sent his son, Jesus ("For God so loved the world that he sent his only begotten son"), we are the recipients of these great gifts at the instant we're born again.

ILLUSTRATION

When an individual suddenly discovers they've inherited tremendous wealth, they learn they are entitled to everything that the wealth provides. They're pleased to discover there is now no limitations or lack. Knowing this gives them great freedom. They begin living in this new reality. To them the old thing is forever forgotten. Newness of life has come.

For out of his great love, being partakers in this wonderful relationship and endearing intimacy, you begin to walk in true holiness. This results in a walk of faith and obedience. Isn't that wonderful? In fact, it's more glorious than mankind can ever comprehend or wrap their brains around. Yet it's true!

Here's a sobering truth worth remembering:
Obedience is never a problem when it's motivated by love. There's a tremendous difference between people who serve God out of love and those who serve him out of obligation or fear. In the churches of today, 95 percent of those who serve God do so because they want God to love them, to find acceptance and approval of their fleshly performances.

READ THIS SCRIPTURE CLOSELY:

1 John 1:1-2
That which was from the beginning, which we have heard, which we have seen with our eyes, which we have looked upon, and our hands have handled, of the word of life (for the life was manifested, and we have seen it, and bear witness, and shew unto you that eternal life, which was with the Father, and was manifested unto us).

Here's what the scripture is saying to you and me: We're showing you eternal life, which was with the Father and has now been manifested (demonstrated, certified, attested to, made evident) unto us.

LET'S READ THIS GLORIOUS SCRIPTURE ONCE AGAIN:

John 3:16
For God so loved the world, that he gave his only begotten son, that whosoever believeth in him should not perish, but have everlasting life.

1) Here's the reason for salvation: *that you might have everlasting life*.
2) Here's the motivation of salvation: *that you might have everlasting life*.
3) Here's the goal of salvation: *that you might have everlasting life*.

John 17:3
And this is life eternal, that they might know thee the only true God, and Jesus Christ, whom thou hast sent.

Eternal life knows God in a unique and intimate way, which cannot be known by mankind in any other way.

1 John 1:2
For the life was manifested, and we have seen it, and bear witness, *and shew unto you that eternal life*, which was with the Father, and was manifested unto us.

How can you show someone on earth what eternal life is, if it means living in heaven, or even having your sins forgiven? Simple—you cannot! But if eternal life is a close, intimate relationship, as we know scripture teaches, then that can indeed be shown or demonstrated to anyone living on the earth today.

ILLUSTRATION

Married couples are easily identified by the outward expressions of their genuine love for one another. We see it all of the time. There's no mystery to it whatsoever. It's clearly seen for what it truly is. They love one another, and their actions display it. It's a no-brainer!

HERE'S ANOTHER EXPRESSION OF LOVE IN SCRIPTURE:

John 13:23
Now there was leaning on Jesus's bosom one of his disciples, whom Jesus loved.

WE KNOW, ACCORDING TO SCRIPTURE, THAT JESUS HAD A VERY PERSONAL RELATIONSHIP WITH THE FATHER, SAYING:

John 10:30
I and my father are one.

Jesus identifies this unique oneness in this next scripture by identifying those who love him, as a direct correlation to his love and intimacy with his father. He implores his father to keep these precious saints in him, that their oneness might be demonstrated in the same fashion to one another in the world, as the Father and Jesus's oneness is and was expressed while he was upon the earth.

John 17:11
And now I am no more in the world, but these are in the world, and I come to thee. Holy Father, keep through thine own name those whom thou hast given me, that they may be one, as we are.

John 17:21
That they all may be one; as thou, Father, art in me, and I in thee, that they also may be one in us: that the world may believe that thou hast sent me.

The distinguishing mark that people will know that you are mine is the love you have for one another. This love was demonstrated openly and without reservation. You love God truly and completely and love humankind truly and completely. They didn't need to be coaxed or forced to make a false show for the masses. Their genuine joy and love for Christ couldn't be contained. It simply gushed out like a river. And it affected multitudes in a positive way. People simply wanted to be part of something that was true and genuine. Don't you? Most Christians are tired of things that are false. That's why you find them constantly moving from church to church. "I'm looking for something genuine, not artificial," they might say.

If the early Christians had an intimate and genuine love for the Pharisees, the Sadducees, and the temple (church), you wouldn't have been able to tear them away, regardless of what you had to offer. They already had something they felt was real, right or wrong. The reality was that after the death of Christ and the infilling of the Holy Spirit in the Upper Room, multitudes were added to the church daily. They knew that this wasn't hype but the real McCoy, something genuine, and they wanted it. They were hungry for it, and it wouldn't be denied them. As a result, multitudes were added daily.

John 13:34-35
A new commandment I give unto you, that ye love one another; as I have loved you, that ye also love one another.
By this shall all men know that ye are my disciples, if ye have love one to another.

The relationship that Christ wants us to have with himself and the Father is the same relationship that he wants us to have with one another. This is the true gospel of Christ, the Word of God in its entirety, the "too good to be true" Good News—the truth that will "make" you free.

THINK ABOUT THIS FOR A MOMENT:

When you hear a message preached about the need to come to God to have your sins forgiven, so you won't spend eternity in hell, here's what's really being conveyed: Your salvation experience is really only one sided. It's all about you and your need to escape a torturous eternity in hell. Great fear has gripped your heart, because you know it to be true. It's also about wanting something without having to give anything in return. That's why Christianity is broken in your life. God wants intimacy with his creation—*you*—*personally*, but you don't want intimacy with him, because of your unreasonable fear. You only come to him when your life is in a mess, never before. You're afraid of him as much as any child whose mother says, "Just you wait until your father gets home." In fact, you tremble at the thought of what might be done to you if you don't. For you, love isn't even in the equation, but fear certainly is. You only dread his wrath if you don't come with a suitable enough sacrifice. Some liken it to being tossed into the volcano to appease the God they think is angry at them. A God of love? Yeah, right!

ILLUSTRATION

We've all heard and studied ancient cultures where people would sacrifice animals, crops, and even children to appease their god's anger.

Jesus did not come to forgive you of your sins. He came to rescue you so he and the Father could forever enjoy intimacy with you and provide you with every good gift from heaven. Show me the anger in that.

HERE'S WHAT THE KINGDOM OF GOD IS LIKE:

Matthew 13:45-46
Again, the kingdom of heaven is like unto a merchant man, seeking goodly pearls: who, when he had found one pearl of great price, went and sold all that he had, and bought it.

This merchant man represents God the Father, who is looking and seeking for goodly pearls: *us*. When he finds us, he goes and sells everything he has to obtain it. The Father sent his son to purchase the pearl that was found in the field. What was the price to obtain this goodly pearl? The cross! The greatest price ever to be paid for anything, but the Father felt it was worth it, so that he might possess it—*you*—in everlasting life. Do you see an angry, vindictive God anywhere in this picture? Neither do I! I only see his love poured out in Christ.

The field is the world. The pearls are those who will accept him and hunger and thirst for an intimate relationship with him and his son. God the Father purchased that entire field—the entire world. He brings salvation to it to gain possession of those precious pearls, the ones looking to find an intimate relationship with their creator.

So when you see salvation as only a way to escape hell, or a means to have your sins forgiven, so you can gain a place in heaven, you've cheapened the cost he paid and the purpose of his coming.

Salvation does indeed forgive sins. In fact, your forgiven sins are cast as far from you as the east is from the west. And the reality of spending eternity in heaven is just as true. But there is so much more. Knowing the only living and true God is the most rewarding and joyful of all God's gifts to mankind. It's something that can be enjoyed in our present human existence and then enjoyed throughout eternity after we depart this earthly vessel.

1 John 1:3-4
That which we have seen and heard declare we unto you, that ye also may have fellowship with us: and truly our fellowship is with the Father, and with his son Jesus Christ.
And these things write we unto you, that your joy may be full.

John is saying the reason he wrote this particular book was to bring you into fellowship with God the Father and his son, Jesus Christ.

The things that we've seen and heard, we bring unto you so that you too can enter into this fellowship. As a result of this intimacy, your joy would be full and remain full all the days of your life.

It was this fellowship, this intimacy, that motivated and moved the early church to great exploits.

CHAPTER 5

LIFE, AND THAT ABUNDANTLY

For the average born-again Christian, intimacy, communion, closeness, or even oneness with God and his son, Jesus, are terribly lacking, almost nonexistent, in their lives. The abundant life they hope to enjoy is difficult for them to comprehend. A few might believe they're entitled to abundant life through their salvation experience, if mentioned at the time of their conversion, but they would be hard-pressed to define it if asked. Generally speaking, the average child of God would conclude that this abundant life they're to enjoy is defined by what happens in their denominational setting: church.

It doesn't take a very sharp or keen eye to see that the relationship of most of God's children attest more to the lack, rather than to the abundance, in their lives.

The average gospel message, which brings the unsaved under conviction in the first place, was never intended to do anything more than just get you saved. Remember when I told you earlier that you can't teach someone something you don't know yourself.

A lot of churches are content with their simplistic view of salvation. Thoughts of giving you more than they feel you can handle seem to them as absurd as giving a small child a very sharp knife. Instead, potential converts are often told disturbing and frightening "not so good news." The pastor usually hammers home our unworthiness because of our sin message. What's quite remarkable is that these men and women of faith actually think they're doing you a favor. By telling you how deplorable your condition is and the subsequent outcome for all sinners who fail to act immediately to receive God's "last chance" salvation offer, they play on a person's greatest fear: going to hell. *Fear*! It'll get D'em every time! It's almost universally used in every church setting and crusade across the globe. You might say that it's their trump card. If nothing else works, fear and condemnation will.

When this type of salvation is received, it isn't with the joy unspeakable and full of glory mentioned in the Bible. Consequently, the experience is lackluster at best and it usually doesn't "stick" for them. How could it, when the primary reason for going to the altar in the first place was because of the fear and condemnation they felt from the message they received. Within a short time, the fear and condemnation subsides and you feel better, but you are actually no better off. It doesn't take long before the next critical crisis takes place and fear is presented once again. You know you'll have to head back to church for another salvation "fix." The dreadful experience endured confronts you again, only worse. This time, you feel condemned because you couldn't seem to keep sin out of your life. In time, you'll leave the church for good, or you look for a different church where the message isn't so condemning.

From the tone of most pastors and teachers, you'd think we didn't stand a chance with God because of our sin. But if we hurry and submit to him right now, "while the time is right," we might just squeak in. Fear!

God doesn't use fear to draw sinners and the wayward to himself. He only uses love. Did you ever notice that love draws, while fear pushes people away. Fear causes panic, but love brings peace. The church wants to push you to Jesus, but Christ wants to receive all who will come, through his undying love for them.

HERE ARE A FEW OTHER TEACHINGS WE HEAR FROM THE PULPIT:

1) That we need to choose Christ so we can live in heaven for all eternity.

2) That if we choose a relationship with Jesus, our names would be written in the Lamb's Book of Life.
3) That the angels rejoice every time a lost and wayward sinner comes home.

These things are true of course, but pastors and teachers have made them the primary focus for coming to an altar. The fear of missing out on these and other things is your motivation to obtain acceptance from Christ. The one thing you seldom hear is that God the Father sent his only begotten son to this earth to restore to you a unique and special relationship, which had been destroyed by sin.

You've not heard how he came to give you everlasting life for the time we have remaining on the earth: an unequaled and unparalleled relationship of eternal importance. Everlasting life is a present tense possession, available for all of God's children. And that possession is an intimate relationship with God through his precious son, Jesus Christ, called everlasting life.

John 10:30
I and my father are one.

WHAT DOES THIS MEAN?

Christ is telling us that he and his father had an ongoing intimate relationship: "that we are one." Christ had this everlasting life relationship with his father while here on this earth, as a human. This same everlasting life relationship is now just as vibrant in heaven with the Father as it was for him while he resided on the earth.

John 17:11
And now I am no more in the world, but these are in the world, and I come to thee. Holy Father, keep through thine own name those whom thou hast given me, that they may be one, as we are.

John 17:21

That they all may be one; as thou, Father, art in me, and I in thee, that they also may be one in us: that the world may believe that thou hast sent me.

There are a tremendous number of people who have an experience with God, but it is not life giving. Neither is it life producing, and it certainly is not the abundant life that Christ speaks about in the following verse:

John 10:10
The thief cometh not, but for to steal, and to kill, and to destroy: I am come that they might have life, and that they might have it more abundantly.

So, if Jesus had a life that was more abundant here on the earth, because he and his father were one, then you too can have that same type of abundant life, *here on the earth*, because you're now one with them through his atonement.

Here's another important thing to note: Though many of God's children read their Bibles, attend church regularly, and live decent and moral lives, they still don't have a unique or intimate relationship with the God of their salvation. They do all these things because it's expected of them as Christians to do, but it isn't life producing or intimate.

HERE ARE THINGS THAT WILL HELP YOU RECOGNIZE INTIMACY:

1) Intimacy with God changes everything in your life.
2) Intimacy with God changes you personally, from the inside out.
3) Intimacy with God breaks down every barrier and wall in your life that separates you from him.
4) Intimacy with God makes flowers bloom in difficult places.

All of these things start to take place with your understanding and knowledge of what salvation is really all about. The understanding and knowledge of what he has done with you, in you, for you, and through you. Now that is totally awesome!

HERE'S A WONDERFUL VERSE. MAKE IT YOURS!

Ephesians 3:19
And to know the love of Christ, which passeth knowledge, that ye might be filled with all the fullness of God.

If I were to paraphrase this verse, it might read something like this: And to completely know the love of Christ, which goes beyond human knowledge, through your renewed and regenerated spirit man. In this, you know that you are filled with the same fullness that is in God, lacking nothing.

TO FURTHER UNDERSTAND, LET'S LOOK HERE:

Ephesians 3:16
That he would grant you, according to the riches of his glory, to be strengthened with might by his spirit in the inner man; that Christ may dwell in your hearts by faith; that ye, being rooted and grounded in love, may be able to comprehend with all saints what is the breadth, and length, and depth, and height.

That you, even *you*, being rooted and grounded in his love, may be able to comprehend what is the breadth, length, depth, and height of the love that he has for you. This is available to anyone who wishes to receive it by faith.

I'm not talking about some man-made theology based on man's intellect or interpretation of faith as the human mind reasons things out. I'm telling you about a relationship with the true and living God—the God of Abraham, Isaac, and Jacob—that can be yours as well.

Jesus said, "My father and I are one, and I long for you to be one with me as I am one with my father."

John 3:16
For God so loved the world, that he gave his only begotten son, that whosoever believeth in him should not perish, but have everlasting life.

Christians stumble by misreading scripture. But the Word of God says we must rightly (or correctly) divide the words of faith.

The primary reason that Jesus came was *not* to forgive you of your sins. The reason that Jesus came was to give you and I everlasting life with him and the Father. It was his original purpose and intent; his motivation, if you will.

You and I weren't the only ones who missed out when Adam and Eve fell into sin in the Garden of Eden. God missed out too! He had this wonderful relationship with his creation, called eternal life, and it was disrupted when they fell. God wanted it back—an intimate relationship with his creation, the ones created in his image and likeness. God didn't fail in his attempt to do just that. The success of the cross proves it. We're the ones who've failed, because we didn't, or still don't, recognize what he accomplished for us. We're ignorant of God and his methods, but ignorance can be changed with truth, if we'll allow it.

The thing about truth is that you have to seek for it with all of your heart. It will reward those who diligently seek after it. Remember: ask, seek, and knock.

Note: You might wonder why I repeat certain parts often. It's really quite simple. In fact, there are three very specific reasons. First, I want to drill truth into you so you *never* forget it, so that you'll use the rightly divided truths of scripture to challenge error when you see it or hear it. Second, that you will use the truths you've learned to teach and instruct others in Christ. Last, it's because most Christians have been indoctrinated with the falsehoods I've mentioned for most of their lives. It takes time to reverse these bad habits and teaching.

THE DEFINITION OF ETERNAL LIFE COULDN'T BE ANY PLAINER:

John 17:3
And this is life eternal, that they might know thee the only true God, and Jesus Christ, whom thou hast sent.

Life eternal is given that you might know the one true God and Jesus Christ, his son.

Intimate relationship is the purpose of salvation, as proven over and over again in scripture. So, if this is the real purpose of salvation, then forgiving you of your sins was *not* the primary purpose. Forgiving you of your sins was just a necessary step in achieving the desired outcome for God: an intimate relationship. If our relationship could have been restored without forgiving you of your sins, then God would have done it. The stumbling block of sin was the problem, so God simply removed the stumbling block. He forgave your sins—once and for all, forever. Intimacy, the primary reason for Christ's sacrifice on the cross, has been restored to those who wanted it and pursued it with their whole mind, soul, and body.

In this light, it's actually much easier to understand sin. Men categorize sin in many ways to fit their doctrinal beliefs. They make some sin seem worse than others, which is a nifty trick of the devil to keep us focused on the wrong issue. If we're focused on that, then we don't consider the weightier matter of our relationship with Christ and God the Father. God sees all sin as the same. He neither differentiates nor categorizes it. To him, sin is sin; plain and simple. Since sin separates us from him, his first order of business is to deal with that specific problem. Because of Christ's atonement, God simply forgives our sin as a trespass and gets on with the real important issue of intimacy.

Again: Sin was barrier between you and him. It was what brought the separation in the first place, so it stood in the way and needed to be dealt with. It was. God's greater mission involved a restored relationship with his creation.

Now, you might be thinking that I'm casual about sin, feeling it really isn't important or worth dealing with. But that is not true at all. I'm not saying that forgiveness of sin is unimportant. I'd be a fool not to know or understand what it did to the human race because of Adam and Eve's choice. It's very important. But it doesn't have the same value as restored intimacy. You've been led to believe that sin was God's primary focus, or the reason that Jesus Christ came, suffered, and died. But it was not!

I believe we need to have the same mind-set as the Father on this issue, as scripture clearly teaches and instructs. Obviously, sin always has an impact on those who continue in it. But those who will seek him in sincerity can ask for and receive forgiveness of their sins. Restoration of the breached wall of separation between you and God brings with it a new and intimate relationship with the Godhead. In this place, you'll find sin to be a thing of the past for you. Once dealt with, why revisit it?

What a tragedy it would be to merely have your sins forgiven and then not participate in the greatest of all supernatural experiences: an intimate relationship with the true and living God. If that intimate relationship does not take place, then you have missed the entire purpose of your salvation.

If your relationship was based upon his love and you really understood the fullness of that love, there would be an immediate increase in all the things that pertain to you concerning life and godliness.

1) Your joy would increase.
2) Your health would increase.
3) Your peace would increase.

4) Your patience would increase.
5) Your faith would in increase.
6) And so on.

All things would automatically increase because grace would be abounding toward you in all things.

THOUGHTS AND QUESTIONS TO PONDER:

1) Have you ever wondered what the difference is between Christianity and other religious organizations or denominations?
2) What's the difference between the Mormons and Jehovah's Witnesses and those who are born again?
3) What's the difference between traditional religious churches and Christianity?

The answer: It's our personal, intimate relationship with God and Jesus Christ.

There are tens of thousands of Christians, who go to fundamental churches all across America and the world beyond, who should know about having an intimate relationship with God. Sadly, they don't have any more of a relationship with him than the churches mentioned above. They're no better off than any *religious* individual trying to appease the gods they say they serve. Acknowledgment of a god will not do it, because almost everybody believes there's a god of some sort. Going to church won't do it, since the houses of worship of all denominations are filled every week. Paying tithes won't do it, because even the unbelievers understand they need to give to support their faith. Teaching Sunday school won't do it either, since we know that all of these churches and denominations have instructors who teach their beliefs.

The difference is the relationship a person has with the true and living God. If you don't have the intimate relationship I've mentioned, then you should question whether or not you've actually received salvation, as the Word of God teaches.

The Word of God says we can know and fully understand how personal this relationship can be.

CHAPTER 6
HOW PERSONAL IS THIS RELATIONSHIP?

After reading the first five chapters of this book, you probably would like to know the answer to the following question: How personal can this relationship be between you and God? It's quite all right to ask this question. I believe all of God's children should ask these and other questions of faith.

Let me tell you that this special, intimate relationship with the true and living God and his son, Jesus Christ, is not reserved for a select few, or even those we might classify as mature or special Christians. Despite the emphasis we place on higher learning and individuals with academic degrees or doctorates in theology, this special oneness or intimacy with the Godhead is afforded the average believer, whether or not they've attained anything in this world that so many deem essential or important for success. It's for the average Christian who comes to the Lord desiring him above all else. I want them to understand that they too can have the same intimate relationship that the saints of old and throughout the ages possessed.

God is no respecter of persons. Period! We all can have this same unique communion, closeness, and oneness with God and the Lord Jesus Christ. He cares nothing about human academic standards, our station in life, or any of the other things we place such value on. In fact, all of the ways of man are foolishness to the Lord. Look at the life of the much loved John the Baptist, who was poor and raised in the desert, knowing only the Word of God, and Paul (formerly Saul of Tarsus), who achieved every academic success and prosperity known in that day, but who was utterly useless to God until he met the master on the road to Damascus. These two people were at opposite ends of the spectrum, yet both developed a unique and special oneness with their creator, the true and living God. In God's eyes, they became equals. We can too!

John 17:21-22
That they all may be one; as thou, Father, art in me, and I in thee, that they also may be one in us: that the world may believe that thou hast sent me.
And the glory which thou gavest me I have given them; that they may be one, even as we are one.

This is what Christianity and being born again are all about. Jesus came to provide it for us. This close personal relationship was severed and broken in the Garden of Eden. God had walked with his creation, Adam and Eve, in the cool of the evening, enjoying the company of his blessed creation. That relationship has once again been restored, thanks to Jesus.

Your sins were in the way, forcing this unholy separation, but he changed all of that with Christ. Your sins were dealt a death blow when he died, having shed the requisite blood as the atoning sacrifice.

John 3:16
For God so loved the world, that he gave his only begotten son, that whosoever believeth in him should not perish, but have everlasting life.

What an awesome and glorious revelation of biblical truth, rightly divided.

The intimacy identified here should be the distinguishing characteristic of every individual who professes to be a born-again child of God.

After our encounter with the Christ of Calvary, our lives should reveal how vibrant, close, and intimate our relationship is with the Lord of glory. You should be talking to the Lord as he'll be revealing himself and communicating with you in this miracle of intimacy. In the world, we might say that "we're loving on each other" all the time.

HERE ARE SOME THINGS THAT YOU AND I SHOULD NOTICE WHEN INTIMACY OCCURS:

1) You'll be walking in his unspeakable spiritual joy (not human emotion).
2) You'll be walking in the pleasure of his company continually.
3) You'll be rejoicing in the reality that you know beyond all doubt that you're the apple of his eye, his precious bride.

This is not to bring guilt or condemnation to those who are not presently experiencing any of these. My purpose is to instruct you and lift you up so that you can see yourself in a completely different light, the light of the revealed Word of God. I want you to see yourself as Christ and the Father see you, to see the relationship that's available to all believers—*you*. At the same time, I need to bring you another truth, the revelation that we've been deceived by another of Satan's lies, which is openly taught in most churches. We've been deceived into believing that God is too high, or removed from us, that we cannot be intimate with him. We've been taught that he is a God of wrath and anger, that we need to do everything within our power to appease and satisfy him.

There are many of you who have a certain knowledge of God, believing within yourselves that he does indeed exist. Many can quote some scripture verses, and others may even be asked to teach a Sunday school class. But they don't really know him personally or intimately. Is it any wonder that you're all stressed out and full of anxiety, worried about many things? As the pressures of life mount against you, you fold up like an accordion, and Satan loves it. All because you don't have a vibrant, intimate relationship with the one who sits above all things.

The one thing that separates the born-again Christian from any "religious" person is the intimate relationship afforded us with God and his son, Jesus Christ, because of our salvation experience.

HERE'S WHAT YOU CAN EXPECT WITH THIS GLORIOUS RELATIONSHIP:

1) It gives you identity.
2) It gives you security.
3) It gives you sanctuary.
4) It gives you safety.
5) It gives you assurance.
6) It gives you confidence.
7) It gives you peace of mind.
8) And best of all it, gives you Son-ship.

There are multitudes of Christians who don't have these things, or at least don't believe they are theirs to possess. They find that life is a constant struggle for them, wanting to believe there's actually more to their salvation than what they've experienced thus far. It's a hindrance to their faith not to walk with confidence in these areas.

I may not have all of the answers, but there's one thing I know, and that is who I am in Christ. I have yet to unlock every door, but these questions have been answered in my life. They can be answered in your life as well.

God loves me! Say it with me: "God loves *me!*" Whether you have an emotional feeling when you say it doesn't matter. It's true! He's given me all that he has and all that he is. All of his promises have been given to *me*, and he desires for me to walk in the knowledge and authority of all, everything, he's given me through his son, Jesus Christ. This is what salvation is all about. Trust me, it's glorious! Having an intimate relationship with the God of all creation—who could imagined such a thing? But it's true! Praise God, it's true!

Have you ever wondered how it was that the early Christians could die for what they believed in? Wasn't it because of the very intimacy I've been telling you about? In the light of this intimacy, it becomes much easier to understand. Wouldn't you agree?

CONSIDER THESE QUESTIONS:

1) Do you suppose these martyrs went to their deaths willingly because of the religious doctrine of that time, their temple or church, or even man's theology?
2) Would you be willing die for the sake of attending the same church that Mom and Dad went to?
3) Would you consider death for the sake of a set of rules and regulations mandated by the church?

I say *no* to all! These martyrs went to their deaths willingly because of the intimate relationships they had with the living God. They possessed more than a religious experience or the influences of mankind. They possessed, in fullness, the Lord God of Israel, in a close, personal, and unique relationship of oneness.

The horrors they experienced can hardly be imagined today, here in America, but they happened as scripture and history record. Their deaths were for the entertainment of Roman officials and citizens alike. Men and women were impaled on large stakes, boiled in oil, or covered with tar and lit on fire along the Roman road. They were mauled to death by lions and other wild beasts. They were tied to four horses and then torn to pieces, all while very much alive. Yet none cried out for mercy. Instead, they sang songs of their faith. Nero was quoted as he covered his ears screaming, "Why must these Christians sing?"

It is recorded in the history of the early church that Roman citizens would literally jump over the walls and run out into the arena, shouting, "I want to be a Christian," because of the joy and peace they witnessed these saints of God displaying on their faces as they were slaughtered, a peace that passed understanding. Could they renounce their Savior and Lord, even at a time like this? Not a chance! Their personal, intimate relationship with the living God was worth dying for.

Now, let's take a good look at Stephen:

Acts 7:54-56
When they heard these things, they were cut to the heart, and they gnashed on him with their teeth.

But he, being full of the Holy Ghost, looked up steadfastly into heaven, and saw the glory of God, and Jesus standing on the right hand of God, and said, behold, I see the heavens opened, and the son of man standing on the right hand of God.

Matthew 26:64
Jesus saith unto him, thou hast said: nevertheless I say unto you, hereafter shall ye see the son of man sitting on the right hand of power, and coming in the clouds of heaven.

Mark 14:62
And Jesus said, I am: and ye shall see the son of man sitting on the right hand of power, and coming in the clouds of heaven.

Here's something very important and well worth noting. Don't miss it! In the above scriptures, it says that Jesus is sitting at the right hand of the Father, and yet in this one spectacular instance (Acts), it says that Jesus, the son of man, is *standing* on the right hand of the Father. Why is Jesus standing, you might ask? Jesus stood, giving honor to Stephen because he was in a personal relationship with this man of God through intimacy, the very same intimacy he wants to have with you and me.

HERE'S ANOTHER EXAMPLE:

Acts 9:4-5
And he fell to the earth, and heard a voice saying unto him, Saul, Saul, why persecutest thou me?

And he said, who art thou, Lord? And the Lord said, I am Jesus whom thou persecutest: it is hard for thee to kick against the pricks.

Take notice: Jesus did not ask Saul why he was persecuting his people. He said, "Why are you persecuting *me*?" Jesus was taking the persecution of his people by Saul very personally.

Matthew 5:11-12
Blessed are ye, when men shall revile you, and persecute you, and shall say all manner of evil against you falsely, for my sake. Rejoice, and be exceeding glad: for great is your reward in heaven: for so persecuted they the prophets which were before you.

Why should you rejoice and be exceedingly glad when these things occur? Because God takes the persecuting of his people personally.

After having lived these many years, beholding the condition of the church I have witnessed today, I believe that the first-century Christians had a much better relationship and intimacy with God than do most twenty-first-century Christians. What's missing? Obviously, it's the oneness they had with their Savior; the personal, intimate relationship.

How many people do you know who would be willing to die for what they have in Christ today? You can seldom tell the difference between the children of God and the children of the world. We don't stand out, or apart.

SEE IF YOU AGREE WITH THESE STATEMENTS:

1) Christians have the same diseases and afflictions as unbelievers.
2) Christians have the same social problems and issues as unbelievers.
3) Christians worry and fret about the same unimportant things as unbelievers.
4) Christians have the same negative attitudes and mind-sets as unbelievers.

When the World Trade Centers were destroyed on 9/11, many, if not most, of God's children were just as terrified and fearful over what was taking place as the ungodly were. If you stood them side by side, you could not tell even the slightest difference between them. It should not be so.

THE WORD OF GOD SAYS THAT PERFECT LOVE CASTS OUT ALL FEAR:

1 John 4:18
There is no fear in love; but perfect love casteth out fear: because fear hath torment. He that feareth is not made perfect in love.

I'll be the last one to suggest that you'll never have any difficulties in life once you experience an intimate relationship with Christ, nor should we be unconcerned about things taking place in our world today. Trouble abounds all around us, and we can be adversely impacted by many of these things simply because we're still in this world. But we should not be discouraged or unduly concerned. We are the children of the Most High God, children of the King. He is our refuge in times like these. All of his covenant promises are our promises to believe and receive. Because we have this unique, intimate relationship with God, we can look forward with eager anticipation and great joy to the things coming in our future. It's our testimony to a lost and dying world. We are both salt and light.

Having intimacy with God gives us the rare privilege of being ambassadors for him.

The world needs him desperately, especially now, and we are the voice he'll use to reach them. Be of good cheer, he has overcome the world.

1 John 5:13
These things have I written unto you that believe on the name of the son of God; that ye may know that ye have eternal life, and that ye may believe on the name of the son of God.

It says here, "that ye may *know* that ye have eternal life."

IT'S NOT:

1) Hoping you'll have a relationship with Almighty God
2) Hoping you'll be going to go to heaven when you die
3) Hoping that you'll be accepted
4) Hoping that things are all right between you and him

BUT RATHER, THAT YOU MIGHT KNOW THESE THINGS:

1) That you hear from God according to his word
2) That you have a unique fellowship with God
3) That you have a special relationship with God
4) That you can walk in the cool of the evening with your creator
5) That you can have intimate talks with God and him, with you

If you do not already have these things occurring in your life, then something is terribly wrong with your relationship with God. Essentially, your walk with Christ is hamstrung. Someone who's hamstrung is only able to hobble around with the few tidbits of truth they have. When your spiritual strength is depleted, you become a spiritual cripple.

I wished people realized how debilitated they are in this world when they don't know the truths of the scripture concerning our privileges as children of God. There's an old adage that says, "What you don't know, or haven't learned, you can't apply." As a result, you cannot experience victory in your life in any area where truth is not learned or revealed.

Scripture admonishes us to know these truths. How can we have something when we don't even know what to ask him for? He's given it and everything else we need to live victoriously here on this earth.

1 John 5:14
And this is the confidence that we have in him, that, if we ask any thing according to his will, he heareth us: And if we *know* that he hear us, whatsoever we ask, we *know* that we have the petitions that we desired of him.

So, do you know these things? You should! There should be this special *knowing* in your heart. It comes with truth and revelation—a renewed mind. Remember, it isn't God's fault if you do not know. He's made knowing available to all.

It's a dark and foreboding world, but we can have a relationship with him in this darkness.

CHAPTER 7
RELATIONSHIPS IN DARKNESS

I want to show you a relationship in darkness. Paul had just received a vision to go to Macedonia because there were those who needed help. He and Silas were the vessels God was going to use. Paul knew it, so away they went.

Acts 16:20-26
And brought them to the magistrates, saying, these men, being Jews, do exceedingly trouble our city, and teach customs which are not lawful for us to receive, neither to observe, being Romans.
And the multitude rose up together against them: and the magistrates rent off their clothes, and commanded to beat them.
And when they had laid many stripes upon them, they cast them into prison, charging the jailor to keep them safely: who, having received such a charge, thrust them into the inner prison, and made their feet fast in the stocks.
And at midnight Paul and Silas prayed, and sang praises unto God: and the prisoners heard them.
And suddenly there was a great earthquake, so that the foundations of the prison were shaken: and immediately all the doors were opened, and everyone's bands were loosed.

Special emphasis: Please listen closely to what's being said here. This is foundational insight to those who want all that God has to offer them.

This account of Paul and Silas reveals the kind of intimate relationship they had with Christ. In the darkest part of the night, in the darkest part of the prison, while others cried aloud to a god they felt had deserted them, Paul and Silas knew precisely who their God was, that he resided in fullness within their spirits. No one forced them to sing or give praises. This situation didn't seem like the place to do that. They were compelled to sing because they knew who their God was. They knew God had called them to Macedonia through the vision Paul received. Their spiritual cup was running over. The pain from the public beating was surely there, but it didn't hold a candle to the glory of the risen Lord that dwelt within them.

Christians cry in anguish when they find themselves in the deepest, darkest experience of their lives, but not these two godly men. These two "ordinary" men of God saw no reason to lament in their situation. They set about glorifying the master of their souls. Oh, the glory of serving Christ, even in this terrible place. They didn't sing or praise God silently like good Christians think they should when persecuted. These men started out loud and got louder. I'll bet that if they hadn't been in stocks, they would have been dancing up a storm. That, dear friends, is victory, in the midst of a terrible situation. The earthquake happened because it had to happen. It was the result of godly intimacy. The devil would love to have brought them low by the circumstances. But circumstances couldn't hold back the flood of praise waiting to burst forth. And burst it did, like a tsunami, praise upon praise, glory after glory. It wasn't a quick "Thank you, God, that I get to suffer for you." No sir. They couldn't get these guys to shut up.

WHY AREN'T YOU SINGING OR DANCING IN THE MIDST OF YOUR TROUBLE?

1) Is there nothing you can find to sing about?
2) Is there nothing you can find to shout about?
3) Is there nothing to even dance about?

In most cases, the average Christian today would be in a state of deep depression, or a state of despondency and despair. They would be complaining to God big time about the terrible situation that was taking place in their lives, simply because they have obeyed his voice to "come to Macedonia."

Perhaps they would sing, but it would be a dirge to those listening. It would grow tiring to those forced to listen. You've probably sung such a chorus: "Oh, woe is me." We've all done it at one time or another. We want others to feel our pain, so the chorus gets louder and louder. "I'm just suffering for Jesus," they would exclaim.

I'll just bet that Paul and Silas were suffering sufficiently because of the torture, though you'd never have known it by the praises that kept pouring forth. Their suffering was drowned out with their melody of praises and worship. This praise was heavenly music to the ears of everyone around them.

ASK YOURSELF A COUPLE OF QUESTIONS:

If you found yourself in circumstances such as theirs, what would you do? What if you were placed in a filthy prison because of your faith, or were severely beaten because of it; would you sing?

If you think you could sing in the midst of such trouble, I would be interested to know why. Multitudes of Christians wouldn't sing under any circumstances, even with fewer problems. Most would simply hang up their spurs and quit. Hard things demand hard choices. Remember, John 6:67 says, "Then said Jesus unto the twelve, 'Will ye also go away?'"

If you study scripture, you'll quickly discover that many godly men and women went to their deaths. They were never delivered from their trouble. But it certainly didn't make them stop singing. That's why Nero couldn't understand these Christians. He was accustomed to hearing pleas for mercy and deliverance, not this.

Paul and Silas sang with no expectations whatsoever of being delivered. These men of God didn't need deliverance, they already possessed it. What's Satan going to do with people like these? Nothing!

Acts 16:26-28
And suddenly there was a great earthquake, so that the foundations of the prison were shaken: and immediately all the doors were opened, and everyone's bands were loosed.

The foundations of the prison were shaken and all of the doors were flung open. Every stock and the bands of those in prison were loosed, falling to the ground; but no one left.

Acts 16:27
And the keeper of the prison, awaking out of his sleep, and seeing the prison doors open, he drew out his sword, and would have killed himself, supposing that the prisoners had fled.
But Paul cried with a loud voice, saying, do thyself no harm: for we are all here.

IMPORTANT ISSUES TO THINK ABOUT:

1) No one was delivered during or after the singing.
2) No one was looking or even expecting to be delivered or to escape.
3) No one was singing with expectations of favorable treatment or deliverance from their captors.
4) No one was singing to have their needs understood or met.

These men of God sang because of their relationship with Christ. They sang and worshipped because they wanted to express their great love for God. They wanted to exalt the presence of God, even in this horrible place, the place of their suffering. Try that one on for size.

Reading this story can put things into perspective, can't it? By the sufferings commonplace in the world during the time of the early church, we can hardly argue that our problems are somehow worse.

But we generally do. We believe no one has ever suffered as we're suffering now. How foolish a statement is that? When was the last time we saw Christians dipped in oil, impaled on stakes, and used as torches along the roads of Rome? I can hardly even imagine such a thing. But it happened, as recorded by history. You could say they were having a seriously bad day. In spite of this, it says that they glorified their Lord as they suffered and died.

I wonder if this isn't a good time to be honest with ourselves and ask if this is the kind of attitude we have in the midst of sorrow and trouble. Do we sing simply because we are in love with him, just because of our relationship with him? Most Christians praise God because they think he will be moved in the midst of their great suffering to deliver them. To them, singing and praising God is the tool they use to get him to move in their favor; essentially saying, "Get me outta here!" But what happens when he doesn't move as they want or expect? I'll tell you what happens. The singing and all praise stops cold.

The miracle of deliverance actually takes place in the hearts of believers, regardless of what is happening around them. It may or may not free you from your trouble. Millions of martyrs can attest to that. But as the three Hebrew children found out, God walked with them in the fire. They had to go into the fire to see that he was with them there.

If Paul and Silas were praising God just so he would free them from the innermost parts of the prison they were in, they certainly had their chance, along with all of the other prisoners, when the bands were loosed. No one said, "Let's make a break for it." No sir! They stayed put. In fact, the jailer was going to take his own life when he thought they had all escaped. Paul told him not to do it because they were all still there.

You may ask, "Doesn't the Lord want to deliver us from these situations? Doesn't he want to set the captives free?" Scripture says so. Indeed he does, but it is not as you might suppose. He wants to make you free in your spirit and mind first. This is the greatest place of freedom. When your spirit man is made free and knows it, then you can sing and worship him regardless of the circumstances you find yourselves in. You might even sing and worship him on the way to your death.

Consider this: When we only praise God so we can be delivered from our trouble, then the reason for our praise becomes purely selfish. It is for the purpose of getting something instead of giving something. I believe our motive for praise has to go beyond getting our needs met. It should transcend our desires to embrace what he desires.

How many of you came into your relationship with Christ with the wrong motives? It's because you've not been properly instructed in the Word of God: scripture. We think this life we live is all about us, when actually it is all about him. Getting your relationship with God straightened out should be your primary focus. It should be based on fellowship and love, not about what you feel you need.

When Paul and Silas sang, their relationship with God manifested an earthquake. The earthquake opened every door and cast every chain and band to the floor; still no one left. Not only did Paul and Silas not leave, but none of the other prisoners left either.

I'm sure that the prison was filled with a cross section of what we call "low-life" individuals: murderers, thieves, rapists, embezzlers, and worse. But they didn't leave either. Now we really have to ask ourselves, why in the world didn't they leave? I believe that they were witnessing a rare and beautiful thing. They were surely awestruck by the relationship that Paul and Silas had with their God. No one else was singing or worshipping their gods. Just these two men! When the earthquake struck, it left little doubt in their minds that this God, the one worshipped by Paul and Silas, was a mighty God, powerful, and someone to be reckoned with.

LET US BRING IT UP TO OUR TIME IN HISTORY:

I wonder what your response might be if a godly earthquake took place on a Sunday morning while you were sitting in your church. Suddenly, the pews start shaking; the floor is heaving, moving in all directions. The choir is singing and the preacher is preaching. Everyone is wondering what is going on. Do the choir members suddenly bolt for the door, followed closely by the preacher and members of the congregation, some clutching their children? Or is there a sudden awareness of people who are awestruck at what is really taking place? The presence of the Lord is manifested in this place because *someone* is singing praises and worshipping the living God. There is intimacy going on between this individual(s) and the God they serve.

Make no mistake: those who are fearful will run, but those worshipping God will remain.

HOW ABOUT SOMETHING EVEN CLOSER TO HOME? WHAT IS YOUR RESPONSE:

1) When the doctor tells you that you are going to die because of some catastrophic disease?
2) When your spouse tells you he or she wants a divorce?
3) When you unexpectedly lose your job?
4) When the banker tells you that you have been turned down for your emergency loan?
5) When you see no where else to go; no way out of your situation?
6) When your house is about to be foreclosed on?
7) When your car is repossessed by the finance company for nonpayment?
8) When all of hell assails itself against you?

ILLUSTRATION

Many years ago, I was preaching a Wednesday evening message. While I was in the middle of preaching, I discovered that my family car had just been hauled away: repossessed. I knew I was behind in my payments but was trusting God to bring in the necessary funds to help me get caught up. The money never came, but those repossessing the car did. For a moment, I got upset. Here I was, a man of God, doing what he had called me to do: preaching his word. Did anyone care about my predicament? It didn't seem so. This was my prison, and I needed to discover if I was going to sing or not. I chose to sing. I rejoiced that I was a born-again child of God, filled with the Holy Spirit, and had the privilege of being his appointed servant to deliver his message to those gathered. I thanked God that as scripture emphatically states I am above only, resting in Christ fully persuaded that I could trust him in all matters of life.

Did I get my car back? Yes, I did. Thankfully, money was provided so I could get caught up. Since that day, I've never stopped singing when trouble comes. I trust God to handle the situations, and he has never failed me.

How many of you, in situations just like this, begin to praise and worship God? You are not expecting to be delivered or set free, though you certainly would like to be. You're content knowing that God is on your side and that he will remain with you in the midst of your suffering. Your intimacy with him is sufficient, whether deliverance comes or not. You sing and worship because you love him desperately. The incentive you have in moments of trouble like these is greater intimacy with the master. The relationship you have with him is far more important to you than what is happening around you.

2 Corinthians 4:15-18

For all things are for your sakes, that the abundant grace might through the thanksgiving of many redound to the glory of God. For which cause we faint not; but though our outward man perish, yet the inward man is renewed day by day.

For our light affliction, which is but for a moment, worketh for us a far more exceeding and eternal weight of glory; while we look not at the things which are seen, but at the things which are not seen: for the things which are seen are temporal; but the things which are not seen are eternal.

Your relationship and intimacy with God will cause you to praise him for his goodness in the midst of great calamity, or the aftermath of a beating. This kind of relationship weeds out the casual Christian, the onlookers. It weeds out those whose motives are self-centered. You may find yourself alone in the flesh, but in great company with the Lord of glory.

There are generally two groups of Christians: 1) Those who are looking at his hands to see what he will give them, and 2) those that are looking directly into his face to worship and adore him for who he is, who are only interested in a personal relationship with him.

ILLUSTRATION

Petting zoos have animals like goats that are drawn to the fence only by what you have in your hand to feed them. When the food is gone, they're gone. When you get more food, they'll be back.

It is a marvelous thing to have goals and then to go forth doing work for the Lord. It is also wonderful to see the manifestation of all the exciting things he is able to do, to witness the Red Seas opening, the walls of Jericho falling down, and the mouths of the lions being shut before your eyes—to walk in victory.

Walking in victory is easy. Having sufficient finances and a good-paying job is easy. Having a nice home with beautiful furnishings is easy. Having no sickness to deal with in your family is easy. Having a happy home with a loving family is easy. But when everything is quickly falling apart in our lives and seems nothing is beautiful or easy, what do you do? Here you are with your backs bloody and lacerated from the severe beatings, and you know you're standing at the threshold of death's door, thinking, what's next? Will your personal relationship with him get you through and cause you to sing because of his goodness and his mercy? Or will you run from him?

I always remember Job at times like these. He was a godly man and was blessed in all things. He had a large family, with many possessions, with many friends, and in good health. Life for him was exceedingly good. Then in a moment of time, everything was gone, yet he did not forsake God, nor, as we learned, had God forsaken him.

REMEMBER THIS:

We will all experience troubles and difficulties in our lives and in the world in which we live. Scripture tells us so. If you were to lose everything that God has given you, or granted to you in this life, you would still retain the most important thing of all. The one thing that can never be taken from you is your relationship with him. Christianity is not about what you have or possess on the outside. It's about the things you possess spiritually, which can never be taken from you: your personal relationship with God and the Lord Jesus Christ, which is real eternal life.

REHEARSING IT ONE MORE TIME:

John 17:3
And this is life eternal, that they might know thee the only true God, and Jesus Christ, whom thou hast sent.

If you don't have an intimate relationship with God, which will sustain you through any catastrophic situation such as a divorce, major illness, or financial disaster, then you quite literally have no hope. You've missed the purpose of your relationship with Christ, which is the most vital experience that you will ever have in your human existence.

Most people equate their salvation with accepting Jesus Christ as Savior and the work that follows. From this point, they're taught to involve themselves in the work of the church, to become faithful and good servants for God. Things like helping in a variety of ministry efforts are therefore encouraged because, as they say, "God is pleased with such activities." Actually, it only provides more bodies for the work, which pleases the pastor and members of the congregation. They might further state that it helps take the "burden" off of those who are already overworked in serving others. They are told that suffering through ministry enhances their Christian experience. Then perhaps Martha should have been glad to see Mary sitting at the feet of Jesus, yearning to know more about her master. That, as we read, wasn't true at all. Martha was angry

HERE ARE SOME OF THE THINGS PEOPLE EQUATE WITH SALVATION:

1) Now that you are saved, you'll need to do something important besides just sitting in a pew listening to sermons.
2) Most people equate their spiritual worth according to what they can achieve or get done for God.
3) Most consider their value to God in the number of souls that they win to Christ.
4) Most believe that church attendance and performing rituals garners the favor of God.

This is the pervading message delivered from pulpits all across America and the world. In fact, every type of denomination known to man teaches these very same things, and they all require service from their flocks.

HERE'S SOME TRUTH TO CHEW ON:

The thing you're going to be held accountable for from God is your personal relationship and intimacy with him—nothing more and nothing less. God will hold you more accountable for your relationship with him than how many souls you've won to him. He will also hold you accountable for what he means to you personally than anything you've ever done for him, purportedly in his name.

YOU CAN BE SURE ABOUT THESE FOUR THINGS:

1) God is after you to give you his best.
2) God is after your heart, that it might be changed completely.
3) God is after your surrendered will, that he might be everything to you.
4) God is after your commitment to him, *not* what you can do for him.

It is a wonderful thing to be in his service, to reach out and touch the lives of other people for his sake. But service, in the eyes of God, is not a substitute for intimacy.

Knowing God must be the heartthrob of your existence, and intimacy must be the reason you serve him.

Remember, there can never be freedom in Scriptural error.

CHAPTER 8

NO FREEDOM IN ERROR

There is much talk about freedom these days: freedom of speech, freedom of choice, freedom of religion, and so on. But real freedom in the spirit and ultimately the flesh comes only with truth. This truth only makes you free when it is received in the true context of what God is trying to teach us in scripture, rightly divided, not man's misguided interpretation, or intellect. How do I know that? Well, by firsthand experience certainly, since no one knows everything in the beginning, or up front. We mature over time, studying the scripture, gaining insight and revelation, understanding along the way with the invaluable assistance of the Holy Spirit. When lessons are learned, we pass that information on to others through our preaching and teaching, so they too can be victorious in all things. You can never be made free in things you've never been taught or by refusing to believe the truths you've been properly taught. Don't let the devil steal precious truths that make you free. Bondage is never pleasant.

So then, truth does not *set* you free, as so many teach. Scripture says, "The truth shall *make* you free." There is a tremendous difference between the two. Being *set* free only makes you free until the next situation occurs in your life that causes further imprisonment, after which you'll need to be *set* free once again. When you are *made* free, you become freer than you ever thought possible. Being *made* free is a permanent condition (or should be, for the children of God). In this place, God is then able, through that freedom, to enlarge you beyond yourself. So that we might truly see yourselves as he sees you: joint heirs with him, victorious in every area of your life, seated with Christ in heavenly places, with every enemy under your feet. Now that's freedom, and the only type of freedom the child of God should ever desire with their whole heart, mind, and soul.

People of faith live far below their proper station in life, in Christ. You do this when you don't know or understand the finished work of Christ in fullness and things provided and placed at your disposal through his death and resurrection. God desires his children to be "above only" in all things, here on this earth, because you're joint heirs with Christ. Do you believe that? I do! That's why I have such an insatiable appetite for the Word of God. The more I learn, the more I get to keep. It should be the same in your life too.

Freedom is a choice. Spiritual freedom is also a choice. It can only pertain to those who truly know the finished work of Christ. Everyone else simply misses out, or at least until they start learning truths as I'm describing to you here.

Though troubles assail on every side, we are not moved by them; we are *made* free. Though in prison, we are not prisoners; we have been *made* free. Paul and Silas were in prison, but they knew they had been *made* free in Christ, so they sang and worshipped. It was easy for them to sing, not a lamenting struggle as most believe. In fact, I believe they sang immediately. They were the freest men in that prison, even though shackled and in stocks. They had just been beaten without mercy; the pain agonizing, but that didn't stop their worship and praise to God.

John 8:32
And ye shall know the truth, and the truth shall make you free.

The past seven chapters have hopefully given you insight into the foundational truths that literally make you free. This freedom is exemplified in this next, ever popular, verse of scripture:

John 3:16
For God so loved the world, that he gave his only begotten son, that whosoever believeth in him should not perish, but have everlasting life.

CAUSE AND EFFECT:

Everlasting life does not come on its own. It is not given to those who only have a casual interest in knowing Jesus Christ. The churches are full of such people. It only comes through the salvation experience by faith. The purpose of salvation is to reunite us with the only true God and Jesus Christ, in everlasting life through intimacy.

John 17:3
And this is life eternal, that they might know thee the only true God, and Jesus Christ, whom thou hast sent.

It's all about focus and emphasis:
The focus of each passage of scripture needs to be understood if we are to rightly divide its meaning. John 3:16 is not so much about perishing as it is our possessing everlasting life—a relationship with God. Sadly, the church has redirected our attention by changing the focus, or the primary importance of this verse, to emphasize our supernatural rescue from the ravages of hell. This is true, of course, but it is *not* what God wishes for us to focus on. When the church restates or changes the focus or emphasis of this scripture, it unwittingly minimizes the value of eternal life, deeming it of little value to us now. Instead, it teaches Christians that everlasting life is the "icing on the cake," or reward after we die.

I have taught you a different, greater truth, rightly divided. This truth reveals the exciting revelation that you and I can have intimacy with the God of all creation because he sent his son, Jesus, to earth to rescue us from our sin. God loves restoration. He's been doing it in the lives of countless people since the Fall of Adam and Eve. He is restoring the intimacy that was stripped away because of sin. In doing so, we're to be victorious in every area of our lives because we know and understand the true purpose of his coming. Knowing this, we can then understand who he is in each of us and who we really are in him. In this relationship you now possess, you have the very mind of Christ, which makes you conquer every issue in your life.

Good news, as appropriately defined, must be good in all things; otherwise, it really isn't all that good. Most churches believe, however, that they must first inject you with just the right amount of holy fear so as to bring about the desired response: repentance. They'll tell their congregations that "a little dose of fear is just the right ingredient to drive sinners to the altar, so they can receive the Good News of the Gospel." Fear may indeed drive them to the altar, but there is also a great amount of torment that comes with this fear. The greatest torment you'll have is wondering whether God will accept you in your current *terrible, sinful* condition. So tell me, where is the Good News in all of that?

Little do these well-meaning Christians know about the ways of God. God never drives men, by fear, to an altar to accept him. He leads them there because of his great love for them—the true message of the gospel. He is anxious for them to come unto him, so that he might wipe away their sins, restoring them to fellowship and intimacy. In this glorious place, they forever feast at his table as heirs of the kingdom.

How does he accomplish that? He does so with the "foolishness of preaching" as seen in this scripture:

1 Corinthians 1:21
For after that in the wisdom of God the world by wisdom knew not God, it pleased God by the foolishness of preaching to save them that believe.

SO, GONE ARE THE FALSEHOODS:

1) Fear and torment drive us to Christ and are necessary components of the salvation experience.
2) God rejects us because of our sin.
3) God pours out his wrath because of our sin.
4) No one can truly know God or have intimacy with him and his son, Jesus.

Intimacy is afforded us here on the earth because we have a relationship with Christ and Father God through salvation. Besides, you need it here, in this lifetime, so his truths can make you an overcomer. You won't need to overcome anything when you get to heaven. The work will be finished over there. Christ came that we might have eternal life through intimacy, both in our present lives now and then later, after we have died and passed into eternity.

ANOTHER GREAT SCRIPTURE:

Romans 10:17
So then faith cometh by hearing, and hearing by the Word of God.

Faith comes by hearing and hearing by the Word of God. This is love speaking—love drawing the sinner to repentance, to Christ.

Hearing the rightly divided Word of God (the truth) makes you free indeed. Hearing half-truths places you in greater bondage.

THE BONDAGE OF FALSE TEACHING TELLS YOU THESE THINGS:

1) Salvation is the ticket you need to escape the torments of hell.
2) Salvation is the ticket to getting all your problems fixed and getting you out of future trouble.
3) Though saved, you can never really expect to have a quality relationship with a pure and holy God.

When salvation is presented in this light, fear is the only motivation for people to turn to God. In fact, this is what most people believe faith is for. When things go well for them and they seem to have some semblance of order in their lives, they lose their motivation to serve or worship God. Most Christians view God as a "rescuer" in times of crisis only, not someone they actually want hanging around all of the time. "How would you like having God looking over your shoulder all of the time?" they might ask. Frankly, I love having closeness with my Savior and God the Father.

When salvation is presented in truth, then the joy of having fellowship and intimacy with God overtakes their lives. In fact, it should get better daily as we understand this unique relationship. These people have no trouble serving God and are a bit confused when they hear other people say that God is unreachable and impersonal.

If the church preached the truth, that an intimate relationship with God and the Lord Jesus Christ was the goal of salvation, the church and its people would never tire of intimacy with their creator. They would *never* tire of walking in the cool of the evening with Almighty God. Isn't that why Adam and Eve, and now you and I, were created? Yes, indeed it was and is!

Revelation 4:11
Thou art worthy, o Lord, to receive glory and honor and power: for thou hast created all things, and for thy pleasure they are and were created.

For his great pleasure, all things were created. We're created for his pleasure, not for his service. You were created for his desire to lavish all good things upon those who are the redeemed—his children—not for what we can offer or do for him.

I have heard many of God's people say that he needs us. That is not true! God has never needed servants to perform or do what he wants accomplished. He is self-sufficient in all things and needs nothing. Before anything existed, God was completely sufficient. He created us because it gave him pleasure to do so. In creating us, he now finds supreme pleasure with us, in intimacy and fellowship.

LET ME MAKE SOMETHING ABUNDANTLY CLEAR:

We were created for one purpose: his pleasure. The church cannot comprehend this at all. The church wants to make you servants or workers for God. If you look at Revelation 4:11 again, you'll clearly see the criteria for our existence: "And for thy pleasure they are and were created."

As much as I believe in the purpose for the church, its existence and glory, and I do, the church is nothing more than a by-product of the fall of mankind.

SO WHAT THEN HAS THE CHURCH BEEN CALLED TO BE IN THIS WORLD?

1) The church has been called to be a set-aside group, special and unique.
2) The church has been called to be the remnant.
3) The church has been called to be separate.

Before the church existed, everyone was a son of God. They walked in fellowship with their creator—Almighty God. Whether you believe there were only two people in the Garden of Eden or more than just the two, these people had great fellowship and an intimate relationship with their God. They met with God every single day and walked with him in the cool of the evening—every evening.

HERE ARE A FEW THINGS THESE RIGHTEOUS BEINGS DID NOT HAVE TO WORRY ABOUT:

1) They did not have sins that needed to be confessed.
2) They had virtually no human need that ever went unmet.
3) They never had a crisis or catastrophe for him to rescue them from.
4) They were in constant communion with God.

5) They were complete in him, requiring nothing from them in order to find acceptance.

Just as it was the Lord's original purpose for the creation of man to have intimacy, before the Fall, so too is the purpose of salvation to restore intimacy with mankind, through Christ.

HERE IS SOMETHING SERIOUS TO THINK ABOUT:

If you were to take your prayer life, as it is today, and then omitted all the times you ever asked God for help, what would you have left?

HOW ABOUT IF YOU OMITTED THE TIMES YOU:

1) Asked God to give you direction and meaning in your life
2) Asked God for wisdom and understanding
3) Confessed your sins and faults
4) Repented of your wrongdoings
5) Asked God for healing in your body
6) Asked God for deliverance
7) Asked God for finances
8) Asked God to bring salvation to someone else
9) Asked God to do something for someone else

If you omit just these few selected things from your prayer life, what would you possibly have left to talk to the Lord of glory about? Thought provoking, isn't it?

Adam and Eve had none of these issues, and yet they fellowshipped and worshipped God continually. They had an intimate relationship only with their creator, no church or congregation—just God Almighty. Is that what you have?

Their relationship with God wasn't based on any need. They never had anything he needed to fix for them, which they considered broken. All they had was intimacy, and that was enough. No, they weren't bored. To them, the time passed swiftly. Every waking moment was pure joy to them.

Revelation 4:11 tells us that is why we were and still are created. We have been made for fellowship with him.

It's all a matter of real value and worth when it comes to intimacy.

CHAPTER 9

VALUE AND WORTH

What is the value and worth of anything? Obviously, it seems to vary from person to person.

ILLUSTRATION

I am intrigued when I go to auctions and find out what people are willing to pay for things. Sometimes, a seemingly worthless piece of junk sells for a ridiculously high price, but something far nicer and pleasing might sell for practically nothing.

The truth is, everything has its value. As we have ventured into the light of God's word, we sometimes have to confront some stark realities. I found several things I once thought were irrefutable in my faith but were later dispelled with the proper Bible study and instruction by the Holy Spirit. I personally believe that the truth needs to be received so that the child of God can begin to be *made* free from those errors in their lives that have brought considerable bondage.

One of the many things I heard following my conversion was that I needed to do something for God; the sooner the better. That would keep me where I needed to be with the Lord: in church and active. "God loves *active* church members," they'd say.

I was always trying to find ways to serve the Lord so he would be glorified through my salvation experience and the work I performed. Since those around me in church could see I loved Christ, I was encouraged to continually look for ways to bring him glory. Bringing glory to the Lord, according to the church, usually meant work and lots of it.

HAVE YOU EVER HEARD THESE STATEMENTS:

1) I was told that I needed to be a soul winner for Christ.
2) I was told that I needed to use the talents that the Lord had given me to serve him.
3) I was told that what I didn't use I would certainly lose.
4) I was told that the Kingdom of God needed laborers to do their part in building the Kingdom of God here on earth.

The one thing that I was *never* told was that I needed to have an intimate relationship with God the Father; his son, the Lord Jesus Christ; and the Holy Ghost.

It seemed to make sense that I should do something useful *for* God, since he had done so much for me by saving me from my sins. I owed him big-time, I thought. As a result, and with the help and advice of countless others, I began to search out and seek for those things I felt I could personally do for the Lord—not intimacy, of course, just human effort. Like yourself, I didn't know any better. I assessed all of my talents, wondering what he wanted of me that would bring him pleasure. I questioned myself by asking, should I drive a Sunday school bus, do yard work at the church, help clean the sanctuary? I even wondered if I was being called to be a preacher (or at least a Sunday school teacher). Before being saved, I had been a musician in a band that performed in bars, but it was apparent that there were plenty of musicians on the platform already. Perhaps I could start my own Christian group and win souls for God that way. There was no direction in my life, just confusion.

I have noticed that the church body will tolerate a little time for you to get your spiritual act together, but they soon grow impatient if you don't get involved quickly. "You can't please God by doing nothing," they'll remind you. "Everyone else is doing something, and God is pleased with their efforts, so you'll need to decide how you'll fit in, so God can be pleased with your efforts too."

HOW MANY OF YOU CAN RELATE TO WHAT I'M SAYING?

It was natural, given this kind of help from "well-meaning" brothers and sisters in the Lord, that I began to equate the love of God only by the things I was doing for him. I never did understand that the love of God toward us is really a simple matter of him loving us unconditionally, with no effort or work on our part.

BE ENCOURAGED WITH THESE WORDS OF LIFE:

Romans 5:8
But God commendeth his love toward us, in that, while we were yet sinners, Christ died for us.

As you see in this verse, he *chose* to love us, even when we were completely unlovable and in sin up to our ears. Where is the performance requirement in this (or any other) verse? You can't find it, because there isn't any. If you received Christ on your death bed, never having the opportunity to "do something to please him," you would still be found in heaven rejoicing with the multitudes when you died. You would still be a son or daughter of the Most High God, whether you ever did anything or not. Learn the story about the laborers, and you'll understand what I mean (Matthew 20:1-14).

Let's stop messing up the message by interjecting the things we think and feel are necessary to do to please Jehovah God. It's an insult to what the Word of God teaches. Will you do good works? Of course you will! But the works you'll do will be done out of the great love you have for him, not servitude. Our righteous works are not to please God, who is already pleased, or out of some sort of obligation to him, but simply because of love only.

ILLUSTRATION

We have all witnessed children who perform tasks. They may do the task because it's demanded from them. These children hate the demand placed on them and do so grudgingly and out of the fear of what will happen if they don't.

Another child may have a wonderful and intimate relationship with their parents. They love their parents and they know without a doubt that the parents love them in return. They do things for their parents because of the love they have, expecting nothing in return. Love is sufficiently enough for them. In fact, they look for things to do because of this love. To them, there is no fear, and they do not abhor the task. This child never grows tired and weary, because for them, as scripture states, "love suffereth long."

IN THE NEXT SCENARIO, THE SAME THING OCCURS.

Romans 5:8 tells us that his love has been *commended* toward us. Early on, I began to equate the love of God, as it applied to me, according to whatever things I was doing for him, to please him. I did not realize at the time that I was wrong in the way I was thinking and had been taught. I later learned through his word—scripture—that God actually commended his love toward you and I, while we were still or *yet* sinners, and certainly long before we could ever do anything *good* to please him. How awesome is that? Do you know what that means? It means that he can *never* love us more than what he did when he sent Christ. If his love is a finished work, then doing things to please him is a moot point, since he already loves us beyond measure. His love is not increased one iota toward us because of the good deeds we perform. Go back to Mary and Martha. He loved them both equally, though it appeared Martha was actually doing more to please him than Mary. Remember, she was "busy doing good things." She must have been dumbstruck when Jesus told her that Mary had actually chosen the better part—developing a relationship and intimacy with him. It has the same effect on Christians today as it did Martha some two thousand years ago. I'll tell you something:

Martha didn't like the message she received from Christ. But I honestly think she learned the lesson. Hopefully we will too.

So while you and I were yet sinners, he loved us. When you become born again, his love was still commended toward you after you were saved, even to this very day.

THINK ABOUT THIS PROFOUND THOUGHT:

If you were blessed to have led a million people to the Lord, he could not love you any more. And if you have never led even one person to Christ, he will not love you less. The reason that God loves you is because God is love, the pure representation of unconditional love.

1 John 4:16
And we have known and believed the love that God hath to us. God is love; and he that dwelleth in love dwelleth in God, and God in him.

God does not love you because you are lovely or even loveable. God loves you because God is love. God loves you because he commends his love toward you, even when in deep sin.

GOD LOVES YOU BECAUSE:

1) He purposes or chooses to love you.
2) He desires to love you.
3) His love toward you can never be improved upon, neither will it ever diminish.

He commended his love toward you while you were yet sinners, even while you rejected and were rebellious toward him. He loved you when you had absolutely no heart or longing for him, and while you were focused on doing your own things. If only you could grasp this, it would literally transform your life. Your value and your worth to him are not equated with what you do, not even for what you know or possibly have a desire to do for him. Isn't that a glorious revelation?

Our value and worth are equated to the very fact that we are objects of God's love. You have been chosen to be loved by God, and that is what gives you worth and value. This is the same as when God chose for himself a people: Israel. How he loved these rebellious, stiff-necked, ever whining and complaining people. Through it all, he loved and cared for them. What a great truth you are learning here. Please never forget it.

HERE ARE SOME LEGITIMATE QUESTIONS WE SHOULD HONESTLY ASK OURSELVES:

1) How many Christians relate their value and worth to the things they do for the Kingdom of God?
2) How many Christians relate their value and worth by the number of souls that they win to Christ?
3) How many pastors relate their value and worth to the size of their church building and congregation?
4) How many Christians relate their value and worth to the ministry that they are involved in or doing for the Lord?

It makes you think, doesn't it? These things don't give you value and worth in God's eyes. The real tragedy is that you have missed what Mary found so easy to understand and long for. The thing which gives you value and worth is that God loves you uniquely and wants to have the kind of relationship with you that will surpass anything you could have ever hoped for. It is in this place—intimate relationship—that we, as children of God, come to a place of complete security, assurance, and confidence in him.

When you believe that it's the things you've done that bring value and worth to your life in Christ, you are walking in great error. This results in a false and unrealistic hope.

Revelation 4:11
Thou art worthy, o Lord, to receive glory and honor and power: for thou hast created all things, and for thy pleasure they are and were created.

We were created to bring pleasure to God. I love that more than words can express. That we, as the heirs of salvation, are blessed to magnify, glorify, and bless the Lord our God. This is enough to satisfy me throughout eternity. I shall never tire of it. Heaven's breath is the praises of the redeemed.

The next couple of scriptures are examples of what many of God's children proclaim while in a church setting or other venues, when singing songs of faith. First of all, most are sung during times of great emotion, because of the setting they find themselves in. The praises sung in these psalms are far different from any outward emotional proclamations. These are songs sung from the pure heart of someone in love with their Lord.

Without a genuine, heartfelt love for God, any words we say, or any praises and songs we sing, which we honestly think glorify God, are simply empty words and emotions. In our humanness, we think God is well pleased with such things, though he is not. We think our human expressions, manifested in these ways, are faith.

Psalm 103:1-2
Bless the Lord, o my soul: and all that is within me, bless his holy name.
Bless the Lord, o my soul, and forget not all his benefits.

Psalm 104:1
Bless the Lord, o my soul. O Lord my God, thou art very great; thou art clothed with honor and majesty.

ILLUSTRATION

Many church people love to attend Christian music concerts; they often find that they can get "caught up" in the emotion of the moment. The concert generally starts with a proclamation from the promoter or musical group, of having great expectations of a mighty "move of God" during the concert, much as one might expect in a large organized crusade. The musicians know that as leaders of this event, they have an obligation to help nurture the crowd's emotional participation. If successful, the attendees start to experience a groundswell of emotion, which they believe to be a true and genuine setting for worship. They attribute this to the move of God they've been expecting from this event, which is supposedly why most have come in the first place. During the concert, the multitude of frenzied people, fanned by the flames of their collective emotions, begins to unleash these emotions in a variety of ways. The result is much weeping, loud chanting, exalting, praising, and collective singing out to God. The concert ebbs and flows, as a mighty sea, with this great human emotional surge. The attendees feel they are in the very presence of Almighty God and know that they have pleased him with their emotional display, or "worship."

Though these people believe strongly that this is what true worship is all about, many of them have no real connection with Christ or the Father born out of intimacy. Their love for God is questionable. It seems that they love the opportunity to make a public display with others who are just as emotional.

The psalms you just read do not relate to that type of behavior at all. Instead, they speak about a person's oneness with Almighty God as expressed in genuine love toward him in these ways:

1) As you praise him
2) As you worship him
3) As you glorify him in your thankfulness, remembering all of his benefits

God is literally blessed and knows you love him in the way he finds most pleasing.

You might say there is no difference. Praise is praise and worship is worship, but there certainly is a difference. The telltale difference can easily be seen by what happens immediately after a concert or the days following. Little has changed in the lives of the majority of these concert goers. They generally don't experience a life-altering change in their relationship with God because of the concert. They simply go back to the lives they led before the event.

Genuine love for God transcends simple human emotion or a display of emotion. It is deeper than most will ever realize. It isn't a onetime experience but a lifestyle change for the true lover of God. They don't need to make an open show of their love for him through their emotions. Their love transcends emotion and their five senses. They love him deeply because they have intimacy with him. These people know of all his benefits to them through salvation, desiring and longing to remain in his presence because of his great love for them. They don't sing to get God to move or to acknowledge their efforts. They sing because their hearts compel them to.

As an heir of salvation, I enjoy praising, worshipping, magnifying, blessing, and glorifying the Lord our God, in my great thankfulness. It is enough to satisfy me throughout eternity. I shall never tire of loving God. I only hope to love him more. This is within our capacity, as we come to know him in the light of his word, through a renewed mind. To love him in this way is natural for the child of God who enjoys intimacy with him. I believe that heaven's breath is the praises of the redeemed to their Lord, out of a pure love for him.

MINISTERING TO THE LORD IS THE KEY TO THIS RELATIONSHIP.

Acts 13:1-2
Now there were in the church that was at Antioch certain prophets and teachers; as Barnabas, and Simeon that was called Niger, and Lucius of Cyrene, and Manaen, which had been brought up with Herod the tetrarch, and Saul.

As they ministered to the Lord, and fasted, the Holy Ghost said, separate me Barnabas and Saul for the work whereunto I have called them.

It says in this scripture that these people of faith ministered unto the Lord. What type of ministering were they doing? They were blessing God for all of his benefits, worshipping and praising him in their thankfulness. They magnified him and glorified him as God and for the great love he had shown them.

I wonder how many of God's children actually minister unto their Lord? Many people will say that God needs nothing, because he is God. But the truth is, God does have a very specific need. This is a concept that very few of his children will ever grasp.

God created you for his pleasure. He also created you so that he could commend his love toward you. Anyone who loves so greatly also has a need to be loved in return. So now you know. The need God has is to be loved by his creation—you.

ILLUSTRATION

Adoption is the perfect analogy. A longing couple, with a seemingly inexhaustible capacity to love, open their hearts and home to a child in an orphanage. They long to have a family so they can fully express their love to this child in ways the child could never have dreamed. In fact, they commend their love to this adopted child in every way possible. Their home is now fully complete.

When the scriptures speak of blessing, magnifying, or glorifying the Lord, we're to understand that is his specific need to be recognized and loved by his own. God knows who genuinely loves him (as opposed to those who just claim to). False love is easily identified when people value their emotions and intellect over intimacy.

According to scripture, the true child of God has no difficulty expressing or displaying their love to their God, because they remember all of his benefits to them. God has commended his love to them, and they have responded by commending their love toward him. To them, it is joy unspeakable and full of glory.

So what is it that truly blesses God and fulfills the need he has? An intimate relationship with the Godhead blesses God. We're to minister to the Lord by blessing God for all of his benefits, worshipping and praising him in our great thankfulness.

This should help us understand and appreciate the necessity of discipleship in our relationship with God.

Chapter 10

Discipleship in Relationship

If you were to ask ten Christians what they felt is meant by discipleship, you'd probably get ten different answers. Most of the answers would center on the service they feel they are expected to render unto God through the church they attend. Very few, if any, would ever identify discipleship beyond the confines of a church setting.

So before I answer the obvious question (what is the meaning of discipleship?), let me ask an equally important question: What is discipleship not?

THINGS THAT DO NOT QUALIFY AS DISCIPLESHIP INCLUDE THE FOLLOWING:

1) Discipleship *is not* about a person only having their sins forgiven by Christ.
2) Discipleship *is not* about having just escaped hell through the conversion experience, being born again.
3) Discipleship *is not* about being called a Christian or belonging to a specific church or denomination.
4) Discipleship *is not* about the service(s) we render or are told are necessary to please God.

The word "discipleship" can be best described as an experience that is ongoing or perpetual. It is a word that describes a committed person who chooses to go forward or onward in a particular endeavor. These people set a path for themselves that requires much learning, instruction, and a life commitment toward a specific objective; in this case, a relationship with God Almighty. It means looking and going forward, never backward, delving into a deep, intimate relationship with God through their discipleship experience. It means going on to greater revelations, where they experience "the deep things of God"—all of which have been provided to them through the atonement of Christ. It's a complete lifestyle change.

Matthew 28:18-20
And Jesus came and spake unto them, saying, all power is given unto me in heaven and in earth.

Go ye therefore, and teach all nations, baptizing them in the name of the Father, and of the Son, and of the Holy Ghost:

Teaching them to observe all things whatsoever I have commanded you: and, lo, I am with you alway, even unto the end of the world. Amen.

This was the last communication that Jesus Christ had with his disciples before leaving this earth and entering into the presence of his father.

You need to understand the importance of these precious last words of instruction Jesus spoke before he departed.

READ AGAIN:

All power is given unto me in heaven and in earth. Go ye therefore, and teach all nations, baptizing them in the name of the Father, and of the Son, and of the Holy Ghost: Teaching them to observe all things whatsoever I have commanded you: and, lo, I am with you always, even unto the end of the world. Amen.

The church calls this proclamation the "Great Commission": "Go ye therefore and *evangelize* all nations," is the message they claim is Christ's last mandate for the end time church. But having researched this in light of other scripture, I do not believe this is what Christ is saying.

THE CHURCH HAS INTERPRETED THIS SCRIPTURE THIS WAY, TELLING US:

1) To tell all nations that Jesus Christ came to earth and died for their sins
2) To tell them how they can receive forgiveness through Christ
3) To tell them that if they will believe on the Lord Jesus Christ, they will not perish nor spend an eternity in hell

How many times have we heard it preached to us the necessity of reaching the world before Christ's return? This is especially true when it comes to missions and appeals by the missionaries themselves. "How will they know unless you go?" they'll exclaim.

Upon closer examination, we can see that there is a vast difference between what is actually being said by Christ and what people like to read into the scripture.

Jesus said, "Go ye therefore, and *teach* all nations."

Can't you see that there is a tremendous difference between evangelizing and teaching all nations? The Lord is *not* telling us to go and *evangelize* all nations. He is telling us to go and *teach* all nations.

READ ON:

Go ye therefore, and *teach* all nations, baptizing them in the name of the Father, and of the Son, and of the Holy Ghost: *Teaching them to observe all things whatsoever I have commanded you.*

The Word of God tells us emphatically to go and *teach* all nations, not to evangelize them. Because of this error, I believe that the method of *evangelism* the church has chosen to reach the world, instead of teaching the world, does a disservice to the multitudes of people they actually think they are helping. The church of the past several decades and today has set their minds and course on evangelism only.

PERSONAL ILLUSTRATION

I recall a Sunday morning, a number of years ago, when I preached at a Methodist church in Madras, India. Before the service, I was reminded that their culture was considerably different than our own, which I acknowledged.

Because this was a Methodist church, I had assumed that they knew some of the basics or fundamentals of Christianity concerning salvation. As I preached, however, I saw that a great many of those in attendance looked at me as though I were from a different planet entirely, speaking something completely foreign to them. The pastor was upset and so were many of the people who had come, though I did not understand why.

I preached assuming they knew what I was talking about, but they did not. The message I preached was offensive to them. Almost 95 percent of those in attendance had the Hindu symbol in the middle of their forehead, signifying their religious culture and belief. Sure, they were in church and had been faithful to attend, but they had no relationship with God. These people had a form of godliness but denied the power thereof, specifically the salvation message that Jesus Christ. proclaimed.

Having experienced this shock, I eventually became aware that the very same thing was happening in the United States of America. Many people have had conversions, but because they have not been taught to become disciples, they were in fact not disciples. They were hearers only, lacking the power therein, just like the folks in India. How tragic!

Many people make a commitment to the Lord, through salvation, but that commitment never reaches the place of intimacy or maturity. They've simply not been taught. They remain stagnant and have no desire to go forward in their faith to seek out the face of God concerning an intimate relationship. So they never attain it. Without intimacy, they face a debilitating future, full of frustration, anxieties, and fears.

I can see it now. An altar call is given and those longing for Christ's salvation come forward. They are instructed to repeat a sinner's prayer to receive Christ, and then the congregants pat them on the back or hug them, telling them the angels in heaven are rejoicing because they've "come home." But that's it. Nothing more is said. So they shuffle back to their seats, feeling good all over. They think they've received it all, but in reality they've missed the greatest gift: the gift of intimacy with their Savior and God the Father.

But how can they receive something like intimacy when those around them, and especially the pastor, know nothing about the experience themselves. They can't teach what they haven't been taught. So the cycle continues, and everybody is frustrated.

When a person is not brought to the place of understanding or does not adequately comprehend the love of God that was commended to them as sinners, the experience is empty. They might know they've been saved, but after a while they find themselves asking, "Is that all there is?" They might even ask others the same question, but they are put off because even these brothers and sisters in the Lord are barely hanging on. Intimacy—what's that?

Just look around. When was the last time you witnessed someone having intimacy with God? If you happen to see an individual who seems to have this "something more" and you are drawn to it, you are quickly advised by your friends to avoid "so-and-so" because they're just Christian fanatics. "And we can't have fanatics running loose in the church. It just disrupts the way we do things around here," they'll say.

The result is that most never enter into intimacy with God. They have a form of godliness but deny the power thereof.

The alternative to having an intimate relationship with God is that most believers are encouraged by their leadership to be more productive in the church setting, where the people are serving God collectively.

"Your relationship with God is something important," they'll confess, but it's been redefined for them. Leaders might suggest that your relationship with God is nurtured and fostered by your involvement in the church, doing things that please God (and, of course, the church). You're told that this is how you'll know God loves you and how you'll feel (through your emotions) God in your life. Then there'll be the cautionary warning. "Don't get ahead of yourself, young Christian, or you'll get into trouble," they might add.

LET ME GIVE YOU SOME REAL, HARD FACTS:

1) Converts are unable to reproduce their faith.
2) You must be a disciple, through intimacy, to reproduce faith.
3) Converts aren't able to train other children of faith.
4) Only disciples are able to reproduce faith and therefore qualified to train children of faith.
5) Religion doesn't change you, relationship changes you. And only Jesus Christ can make that change happen.

John 17:3
And this is life eternal, that they might know thee the only true God, and Jesus Christ, whom thou hast sent.

I'm not here to determine who is and who is not truly born again. That is for the Lord to know. But I can tell you that there is a vast group of people in this country who call themselves Christians who have absolutely no relationship with the one true God, the Holy Spirit, and the Lord Jesus Christ, whom he has sent.

The truth is, there are a tremendous number of professors, but very few possessors, of Christianity.

How can I make such a claim? It's actually quite easy. Most people consider the United States to be a Christian nation, since this nation was founded on Christian principals. This is undisputed. We have a high percentage of people within our borders who claim to be Christians; in fact, the majority claim to be "Christian" here in America; *with a large percent* of these Americans stating unequivocally that they are born-again Christians. A smaller percent claim to be evangelicals, meaning that they are born-again Christians who consider themselves to be "totally committed" in their faith.

If that's so, then what on earth is happening to our country? Shouldn't we be seeing a resurgence of families and businesses reuniting under the banner of Christ? Wouldn't we be witnessing diminishing crime and violence in our cities and streets? Wouldn't abortions cease to exist and prayer once again be offered in our schools? Wouldn't our lost freedoms be restored and our way of life become the envy across the globe once again? Wouldn't our jails and prisons empty out and terrorism be vanquished within our borders? Wouldn't our children and the elderly be safe and protected against all manner of foul and evil intent? Wouldn't our entertainment and music be brought into line and be less morally bankrupt than what we're seeing on our TVs and hearing on our radios? Hollywood, which is but a very small minority, would be unable to rule and reign in the types of filth they currently bring into our culture, if we were a godly nation. America the beautiful is nothing but a foul stench to the world. It spews forth more filth than any other country in the world, as we proudly proclaim ourselves a Christian nation. The list goes on!

So then, what America and the church calls Christianity today is really a lie. We are not the people we think we are, nor do we have the relationship with the true and living God we think we possess. What we profess to be and have is destroying America and the citizens who reside within her borders. I tell you something is wrong, and what is wrong is that we have a tremendous number of people who have been converted, or born again, who have not been taught to be disciples of Christ. They have been deceived into believing that they have a relationship with God, but it's only through organized religion. And religion stinks!

IS YOUR RELATIONSHIP THROUGH:

1) Your tradition(s)?
2) Your church?
3) Your denomination?
4) Your family?
5) An outward appearance of righteous living?
6) An acknowledgment of a higher being?
7) Your knowledge or intellect that God exists?

HERE'S A SHORT LIST OF SOME OF THE GODS WE WORSHIP IN AMERICA TODAY:

1) The god of religion
2) The god of materialism
3) The god of careers
4) The god of lusts
5) The god of sensuality
6) The god of greed
7) The god of money
8) The god of self-righteousness

And Jesus Christ becomes just one more god for mankind to worship.

The reason this is taking place is because the church has never done what Christ commanded his church to do. It is true that the Christian church has gotten multitudes of converts, but precious few disciples. We have no difficulty teaching them to be good church attendees, but we don't disciple them to be followers of Christ, teaching them to observe all things as Christ commanded. Nor do we help them understand the need to make a total commitment to the God of their salvation through intimacy.

The church of today seems wholly content to focus on its own self-appointed calling, which is to win the lost through evangelism. I believe they want people saved, but they don't want them to change too much, to be too holy, so as to become radicals, which are difficult to handle. We have therefore ignored an intimate relationship with God as scripture teaches, deeming it of little value to us while we are here on this earth. We can be as radical as we want when we get to heaven, but not here, not now.

Another prickly point:
Haven't you noticed that we seem to have a tremendous number of people claiming Christianity, especially in America, but who are not Christ-like? They have been deceived into believing they can be one without the other, but it is not true. This deception gives the world the wrong example of what true Christianity is all about.

WHAT WE HAVE NOT BEEN CALLED TO DO:

1) We are not called to make converts.
2) We are not called to make baby Christians.

WHAT WE HAVE BEEN CALLED TO DO:

1) We are called to make disciples.
2) We are called to teach them to observe all things as Christ commanded.
3) We are called to be mentors of the faith.

So when the church finds itself going from place to place, neighborhood to neighborhood, city to city, and country to country, making converts only, we are not grasping the true context of the Word of God. It is great to make converts for Christ, but it is greater still to make disciples of Christ.

Under the laws of this country, it becomes the responsibility of the parents to properly train and instruct their children, so that as they grow and mature, they become, as it were, disciples or true citizens of this country by the laws that govern this nation. Parents become liable if they do not. Anyone who continues to make babies but does not follow up, teaching them responsibility and accountability, is subject to criminal charges.

In the natural realm, that person would be accountable to the authorities for their lack of responsibility concerning that child. In the spiritual realm, we do this very thing over and over again, and think nothing of it, while claiming to do so much for the Kingdom of God and to further our relationship with him.

CONSIDER THIS SCRIPTURE:

John 8:28-30
Then said Jesus unto them, when ye have lifted up the son of man, then shall ye know that I am he, and that I do nothing of myself; but as my father hath taught me, I speak these things. And he that sent me is with me: the Father hath not left me alone; for I do always those things that please him. As he spake these words, many believed on him.

Because of what these Jews were hearing from the mouth of Christ, they became convinced that he was indeed who he proclaimed to be, and it says that "many believed on him."

THESE PEOPLE, HEARING CHRIST'S WORDS, BELIEVED THE FOLLOWING:

1) That he was the Messiah, the long-awaited and promised one
2) That he was truly the son of God
3) That he had come to deliver the nation of Israel
4) That the Father had sent him

The church of today would like to believe that these Jews became followers and therefore converts of Christ. But that is not the case. Why not, you ask? Because believing and accepting are entirely different.

Generally speaking, we Christians think that just because a person says they're a Christian, we automatically assume that they are followers of Christ and have had a salvation or born-again experience. We equate our belief on him as unto to salvation, but that is certainly not true with most people who profess to be Christians.

The stark realization is that they believed on him, yet they were not prepared to receive him as Lord of their lives. They believed on him yet were not changed nor transformed.

Chew on this: *Faith alone does not save you.*

Faith without works is dead if it operates alone. True faith never operates alone. It has works and actions, which identifies or reveals the truth from a lie. See for yourself:

James 2:17
Even so faith, if it hath not works, is dead, being alone.

Believing by acknowledging (false faith) will never cause you to lay down your life for Christ. It is not a true faith, no matter what you think, and is therefore dead.

Believing by accepting, to the extent you are willing to lay down your life for Christ, is *true faith*. This type of faith influences great changes in your life and can be considered *saving faith*.

These Jews believed on him, as the word says, yet were not saved.

John 8:31-32
Then said Jesus to those Jews which believed on him, if ye continue in my word, then are ye my disciples indeed; and ye shall know the truth, and the truth shall make you free.

Jesus, when speaking to them and us today, tells us what is necessary for those who believe.

If ye continue in my word, then are ye my disciples indeed; and ye shall know the truth, and the truth shall make you free.

The word "continue" in the Greek is *"meno"*: me/nw (men'-o); (Strong's NT:3306), and it means to abide in; to stay or dwell in; and to stand firmly upon. So if you hold unto, or adhere to, these truths, developing and growing in the light of them, then you will be his disciples indeed, in truth, or in fact.

SO WHAT HAVE WE LEARNED?

1) Hearing alone is not sufficient to become a disciple of Christ.
2) Believing on the Lord alone does not make you his disciple.

So what does the word "disciple" really mean?
It means to be an adherent, or follower, of someone; a pupil. A disciple is someone who gladly follows a person, accepting the fact that they will be transformed in the process.

IT SEEMS SIMPLE ENOUGH, BUT HERE IT IS ONE MORE TIME:

If ye continue in my word, then are ye my disciples indeed; and ye shall know the truth, and the truth shall make you free.

What a powerful scripture for the true child of God to cling to.

Unfortunately, in the church world today, the word "disciple" has a completely different connotation. Today's Christians believe it is of far greater importance for a convert to be identified with their church's denomination than with the God they claim to serve. If you ask a person what they believe, they'll say what denomination they belong to (e.g., I'm a Methodist, Baptist, Church of God, Nazarene, the Salvation Army, etc.). Who they are in Christ is generally tied 100 percent to the denominational teachings of the church they attend.

Have you ever noticed that when a Christian reaches out to someone, they never want that person to go to any other church? In their eyes, every other church is unqualified because of their doctrinal beliefs. The person in question is convinced by much conversation that they should attend the same church, so they'll receive *real biblical truth.*

Instead of making disciples of Christ, the church makes them disciples of their doctrine and teachings. They don't want their adherents to go far; instead, they enlist them to help grow their denominational church. In fact, it almost seems that the church doesn't want their members thinking too far outside their denominational setting, for fear they'll leave and go to some other church. This is why the church setting is so rigidly structured to keep their people happy. These pastors give them just enough information, teaching, and programs to keep their flock coming back. You'll never find them going to the deep end of discipleship, however, when the shallow end seems so much safer for them.

In any church, to be a believer is a requirement, but becoming a disciple of Christ is not strongly encouraged. Most people in mainline denominations are convinced they need the teachings or instruction of the church. It is implied that being holy is a lifelong endeavor, which most are not spiritually equipped to handle; it is best left to the professionals. They're also convinced that a person needs to have a tremendous amount of theological training in order to fully understand the ways of God. "That's what the pastor is there for," they'll tell you. The "don't try this yourself" mentality is reinforced by the leadership to keep their people spiritually dependent on their church for guidance in all spiritual truths. Watch any religious television broadcast, and you'll see exactly what I mean.

It is little wonder that these educated theologians and doctors of divinity have so little to do with down-in-the-dirt disciples of Christ. In their eyes, we fall pitifully short of being godly or even holy, believing we're unworthy of a relationship with God. They think that it's categorically impossible for ordinary people to know God apart from formal education, or at least having gone through denominational training.

The message we've heard in our churches has left most of God's children bewildered and confused about their relationship with Christ and the Father. But the Word of God is very clear, leaving no "wiggle" room or doubt. We have not been called to make converts. Instead, we have been called to *teach* all nations, making disciples of them.

WHAT DOES MAKING DISCIPLES ACTUALLY MEAN, AS OUTLINED BY SCRIPTURE?

1) Making disciples is drawing people into a total commitment through biblical instruction and through godly persuasion; the work of the Holy Spirit.
2) Making disciples is bringing people into true intimacy with the Godhead, as God desires and commands.
3) Making disciples is helping people commit to a total reliance on Christ, which *makes* them free.

Making disciples through proper training and instructed truths benefits everyone, including you, as the servant of Christ.

In essence, the church has cheapened the gospel for the sake of making converts. We were once a God-fearing nation, but we have relinquished our spiritual birthright, just as Esau did his to Jacob.

When the Word of God is watered down, then everyone thinks they are qualified to call themselves Christians. No longer are we a nation who serves the true and living God. We now bow our knee to every god of convenience that comes along, while still professing to be Christians.

HERE ARE THE THREE THINGS WE MUST DO:

1) We are instructed to lead the lost to Christ.
2) We're then called to teach these converts how to become disciples.
3) When this is accomplished, we're to instruct these disciples in the ways of holiness so they can have intimacy with the God of their salvation, trusting in him only and in every area of their lives.

LET'S TAKE ANOTHER LOOK AT JOHN 8:31:

Then said Jesus to those Jews which believed on him, if ye continue in my word, then are ye my disciples indeed; and ye shall know the truth, and the truth shall make you free.

John 8:33
They answered him, we be Abraham's seed, and were never in bondage to any man: how sayest thou, ye shall be made free?

After Christ says to them, "and the truth will make you free," the very ones who believed on him became offended.

Please allow me a little liberty, as I paraphrase this scripture for understanding and clarity.

Jesus says, "Yes, you believe on me, and even that I am the long-awaited Messiah, which is certainly a good start, but there's something else. In order to be one with me, you must continue in the things I've told you, without wavering. You must abide and remain with me, regardless of the situations and circumstances that come against you, or that you find yourselves in. You'll need to eat my flesh and drink my blood so that others will know beyond a doubt that we are one and the same; that you are truly my disciple."

Some might say this is pretty intense stuff, and I would agree. Is it easy? Hardly! Death is seldom easy. You'll need to die to yourself and your ambitions, but it'll be the most rewarding thing you'll ever do in your human existence. This oneness will help prepare you for the eternity that awaits every child of God and those who long for his appearing. We can start our eternity in paradise with our commitment to be as he is here on this earth. It's such a wonderful journey.

Ask yourselves this: Do you honestly think that heaven will be filled with people who really don't want to be there, or who do not want to possess this oneness with Christ? I don't believe so.

CONTINUING:

These believers in Christ said to him, "We be Abraham's seed, and were never in bondage to any man: how sayest thou, ye shall be made free?"

They already believed the lie, because the stark reality was that they were under terrible bondage and slavery to the Roman government. They weren't free, as they had supposed. Freedom, though desired, was no more a reality for them than it was for the children of Israel when they were in terrible bondage in Egypt.

Christ wasn't talking to them about their humanness, of course. He was talking about their spiritual condition, a realm where no one could enter except Christ, the Father, and the Holy Spirit. In the spiritual realm, they were still under the bondage of and in slavery to sin. These believers of Christ believed a lie and were deceived twice over.

HOW MANY PEOPLE DO YOU KNOW WHO ARE UNDER THE SAME DELUSION? THEY BELIEVE THEY'RE SAVED SIMPLY BECAUSE OF THE FOLLOWING:

1) They had repeated a prayer, which promised them salvation.
2) They signed a card at an altar, which authenticated the event.
3) They had been baptized as an infant in a church.
4) They faithfully attend church.
5) They give financially to their church, or even pay their required tithe.
6) They're involved or help out in some form of church ministry or outreach.

Just as these Jews, many today have been deceived, and the terrible news will eventually catch up with them. They are not disciples of Christ.

Let me ask you: Have you too been deceived?

Continuing in his word is a life-altering experience.

CHAPTER 11
CONTINUING IN HIS WORD

"If ye continue in my word, then are ye my disciples indeed," or perhaps better stated, "Ye are my disciples in *truth*." Reread the scripture with this change and I think you will better understand it.

John 8:30-32
As he spake these words, many believed on him.
      Then said Jesus to those Jews which believed on him, if ye continue in my word, then are ye my disciples indeed; and ye shall know the truth, and the truth shall make you free.

What the Lord is talking about here is something almost totally foreign to most believers. Most Christians today believe it is sufficient enough just to accept Christ as their Savior. They say that if it was sufficient to get them saved, it must be sufficient for everything else.

What foolishness. It's like telling a newborn baby that being born is sufficient unto itself; that they'll no longer require anything in life beyond what they've already received. Who would ever believe such nonsense? Christians do! Unless they're taught the truths of scripture, they'll remain infants until their death.

Well, let me be very blunt and absolutely clear on this issue. The Word of God tells us that it is *not enough* just to believe on Christ. Can't you almost hear the collective groans from Christians everywhere who are reading this book? "What do you mean, it is not enough to believe?" they'll argue.

The Word of God tells us that you must go, a step, beyond believing. Believing is certainly wonderful and necessary for salvation, and it does set sinners free in Christ, but it does not make them disciples.

In order to be a disciple, you must continue (daily) in his word. This is a process that takes time but is not impossible to attain. It is not unlike human education; you get out of it what you put into it. Some will progress faster than others, but it's attainable to all, and yes, in your lifetime. You must have a strong longing and desire to be taught and molded into a true disciple of Christ. This type of person wants to be more than a casual listener to a Sunday morning or Wednesday night message. These precious few will do whatever it takes to nurture this newfound relationship with God, regardless of the cost in time and effort. I know of nothing that can be compared with being a true disciple. It is greater and more rewarding than anything afforded us in our mortal existence. It is, in fact, supernatural.

Psalm 119:73
Thy hands have made me and fashioned me: give me understanding, that I may learn thy commandments.

Matthew 11:29
Take my yoke upon you, and learn of me; for I am meek and lowly in heart: and ye shall find rest unto your souls.

Here's another radical statement: Acknowledged belief is not sufficient either. So if you believe that Jesus Christ is the son of God or know that he died for your sins, it's still not enough.

You must believe it to a point where it produces action and change in your life. As I said, "Faith without works is dead."

James 2:20
But wilt thou know, o vain man, that faith without works is dead?

We have all heard the phrase that "actions always speak louder than words." Well, your faith, or your believing, has to produce actions, because faith, being alone, is dead.

James 2:17
Even so faith, if it hath not works, is dead, being alone.

James 2:19
Thou believest that there is one god; thou doest well: the devils also believe, and tremble.

So you believe that there is one God. Okay, but that isn't anything to shout about. Even devils believe and tremble. Most people think that it's the believing part that makes them a Christian; believing that there is one God. Not so!

James 2:20
But wilt thou know, o vain man, that faith without works is dead?

If, as it states, the devils believe that there is but one God, they are acknowledging the truth. Truth is even acknowledged by devils, though it pains them. But knowing this truth has not freed them, nor have they yielded or surrendered to the truth, nor will it ever free them.

Many believers in God live in total opposition to him. They too have not yielded or surrendered to this truth. They've not made a total commitment to that belief or even advanced to the point where it produces a greater change in them. It's not a reality in their lives. As a result, their life is in direct conflict with God and what the scriptures proclaim. In effect, they are no better off than the devils who believe in God and yet tremble.

So believing in God is not enough. You must yield yourself to those things you claim to believe. Once you've surrendered, your actions start corresponding to that belief, by faith. If you state that Jesus is your Lord, then you'll submit to him as your Lord and master.

Let me make one thing abundantly clear: I am neither saying nor proclaiming that any person who still has sin, or struggles with the many issues in their life, is not truly born again. What I am saying, however, is that there are a tremendous number of people who profess to know Jesus Christ as Lord, but do not know him in intimacy. They know about him, maybe even say that he is the son of God, but these people are in direct opposition and fight against the very Word of God.

You can't just join a church and become a member and then claim that it's sufficient to make you a child of God. But millions do. Since they have not surrendered to Christ, they do not possess true salvation. Their claim to be Christ-like is a lie.

Your life must give evidence of new life in Christ, giving credence to him and the fact that he reins and rules inside of you. You could ask yourself, "If I were arrested for being a Christian, would there be enough evidence to convict me?"

HERE'S A GOOD EXAMPLE:

If I said that the building we were in was on fire and that we would all die if we didn't leave quickly, what would you do? Well, if you really believed what I was saying, wouldn't it produce action in you? Without looking around, you would simply run outside because you knew I was right.

But what about the individual who sits in a pew in church and says, "Oh, I believe; I know that the preacher wouldn't intentionally lie to me." But what if he was not moved or did not take the corrective action necessary? Will his belief save him from coming judgment? Absolutely not!

In our world today, we have millions of people who profess Christianity and the born-again experience, but without the corresponding actions or evidence to confirm its truth, it is all talk. Nothing they've proclaimed is a reality in their lives. It's a fabrication of truth—a lie.

If you remember history, you know that the Jews believed in the coming Messiah, but they rejected him completely when he came into their very midst. They believed in God and knew about the promised Messiah, through scripture and the prophets, but it did them little good. They didn't believe when the opportunity presented itself, which was Christ in the flesh.

And Jesus said to them, "If you continue in my word, then are you my disciples indeed (or in truth), and the truth will make you free."

"So what are you saying, Preacher?" you ask. "Are you telling me that if I profess Christ without corresponding actions, I'm not truly born again?" The answer is revealed in scripture.

I said it before, and I'll repeat it again here: I am not the judge and jury when it comes to determining whether someone is born again or not, but scripture is sufficiently clear on the subject. When your life does not line up with what you say or profess you are, then your life is in direct opposition to the Word of God.

READ IT FOR YOURSELF:

Luke 6:46-49
And why call ye me, Lord, Lord, and do not do the things which I say?
Whosoever cometh to me, and heareth my sayings, and doeth them, I will shew you to whom he is like: he is like a man which built a house, and digged deep, and laid the foundation on a rock: and when the flood arose, the stream beat vehemently upon that house, and could not shake it: for it was founded upon a rock.
But he that heareth, and doeth not, is like a man that without a foundation built a house upon the earth; against which

the stream did beat vehemently, and immediately it fell; and the ruin of that house was great.

Luke 13:25-27
When once the master of the house is risen up, and hath shut the door, and ye begin to stand without, and to knock at the door, saying, lord, lord, open unto us; and he shall answer and say unto you, I know you not whence ye are: then shall ye begin to say, we have eaten and drunk in thy presence, and thou hast taught in our streets.

But he shall say, I tell you, I know you not whence ye are; depart from me, all ye workers of iniquity.

Matthew 25:1-12
Then shall the kingdom of heaven be likened unto ten virgins, which took their lamps, and went forth to meet the bridegroom.

And five of them were wise, and five were foolish.

They that were foolish took their lamps, and took no oil with them: but the wise took oil in their vessels with their lamps.

While the bridegroom tarried, they all slumbered and slept.

And at midnight there was a cry made, behold, the bridegroom cometh; go ye out to meet him.

Then all those virgins arose, and trimmed their lamps.

And the foolish said unto the wise, give us of your oil; for our lamps are gone out.

But the wise answered, saying, not so; lest there be not enough for us and you: but go ye rather to them that sell, and buy for yourselves.

And while they went to buy, the bridegroom came; and they that were ready went in with him to the marriage: and the door was shut.

Afterward came also the other virgins, saying, lord, lord, open to us.

But he answered and said, verily I say unto you, I know you not.

Matthew 7:21-23
Not everyone that saith unto me, Lord, Lord, shall enter into the kingdom of heaven; but he that doeth the will of my father which is in heaven.

Many will say to me in that day, Lord, Lord, have we not prophesied in thy name? And in thy name have cast out devils? And in thy name done many wonderful works?

And then will I profess unto them, I never knew you: depart from me, ye that work iniquity.

Do you think these scriptures are vague concerning this? They are not vague but rather quite clear.

I have not been called to separate the wheat from the tares, which is Christ's alone to do. My responsibility, as a pastor and teacher, is to bring you the truth of his word, if you will hear. Bringing forth the truth of God's word becomes life to the child of God who hears the "too good to be true" Good News, and then become a doer of that word. These people are made free.

Remember, truth alone does not make you free.

CHAPTER 12
TRUTH ALONE DOES NOT MAKE YOU FREE

The Word of God states in John 8:32, "And ye shall know the truth, and the truth shall make you free."

Here's another revelation for you: Truth alone does not make you free any more than saying you are a Christian makes you a disciple of Christ.

THIS IS WHAT'LL MAKE YOU FREE:

It is the truth that you know and understand that makes you free.

Truth doesn't make anyone free!

I've ministered for more than twenty years in churches, over the radio, on television, in this country, and across the globe, and I'll guarantee you that not everyone who ever heard me was made free by the truths I preached. This has been explained by the Word of God. Even the ministry of Jesus, while he was here on earth, proves that truth alone doesn't make anyone free. He ministered to multitudes during his life, and yet he was almost totally alone when they nailed him to the cross.

What I am telling you is true. The power of God is preached unto salvation, and yet people are not being made free by what they are hearing or being taught.

You have to know the truth and accept it as your own before it will make you free.

What does "and ye shall know the truth" actually mean? It means to receive and embrace it, making it a *lifestyle* for you, after which you are promised that it will make you free. It'll change and transform your life forever. Once you taste it, you'll never want anything else. It's heavenly food. We are kept free by constantly renewing our minds to these revealed truths.

Christ was attempting to give these Jews something that would favorably change their lives forever. But how did they react upon hearing his words in John 8:30-31? They were greatly offended that he would insinuate they weren't as free as they supposed. Obviously Christ wasn't talking about their freedom as to their flesh, but they couldn't discern the difference and became stiff necked. In defense of what they believed, they dredged the past to proclaim they were Abraham's seed and therefore as free as they ever needed to be, because of him. What foolish things we say in defense of our position and condition.

John 8:33
They answered him, we be Abraham's seed, and were never in bondage to any man: how sayest thou, ye shall be made free?

Obviously these Jews couldn't understand their spiritual condition or their need to be made free by the truths Christ was trying to teach them, but they certainly needed a refresher course in what they called freedom. Even though they were from Abraham's seed, the Jewish nation had spent much of their existence in bondage to others because of the choices they made. They weren't free at all. In fact, they were bankrupt in the freedom department, both in the world and certainly spiritually.

When Christ told them that they needed to completely surrender their lives to him and become true disciples, they were put off. You might say that they actually liked what they had become. Change is difficult, but with the right mind-set, trusting the Word of God in all things, it can be done by faith.

You and I, like the Jews of antiquity, acknowledge that there are areas in which we need Christ and are even comfortable letting him have control over those areas. But when challenged to change the areas we're already comfortable with in the flesh, we want Christ to mind his own business. We're put off.

There are a great many of God's people who are just exactly like this. They will give God their Sunday mornings, but they won't give him their Mondays, Tuesdays, Wednesdays, Thursdays, Fridays, or Saturdays.

You can see them in your churches. Willingly, they'll give God their gifts and tithes, but they never seem to give God what he truly longs for: their personal lives in intimacy. Devotions are fine to give God, but most don't want God to interfere in their work or careers. They'll have time for a little prayer, but letting God deal with their rebellious children, or besetting sins, well, that's something entirely different.

CHRIST HITS THE NAIL ON THE HEAD:

John 8:34-37
Jesus answered them, verily, verily, I say unto you, whosoever committeth sin is the servant of sin.

And the servant abideth not in the house forever: but the son abideth ever.

If the son therefore shall make you free, ye shall be free indeed.

I know that ye are Abraham's seed; but ye seek to kill me, because my word hath no place in you.

Don't forget, Jesus was still speaking to those who believed on him. Here's the point and honest truth: Some of these very people who believed on Jesus were going to be the ones joining with the scribes and Pharisees, calling to crucify him.

Jesus says it right here in this scripture: "Ye seek to kill me." Why? "Because my word has no place in you."

CHRIST PRESENTS A SCATHING REBUKE OF THESE BELIEVERS:

John 8:38-47
I speak that which I have seen with my father: and ye do that which ye have seen with your father.

They answered and said unto him, Abraham is our father. Jesus saith unto them, if ye were Abraham's children, ye would do the works of Abraham.

But now ye seek to kill me, a man that hath told you the truth, which I have heard of God: this did not Abraham.

Ye do the deeds of your father. Then said they to him, we be not born of fornication; we have one father, even God.

Jesus said unto them, if God were your father, ye would love me: for I proceeded forth and came from God; neither came I of myself, but he sent me.

Why do ye not understand my speech? Even because ye cannot hear my word.

Ye are of your father the devil, and the lusts of your father ye will do. He was a murderer from the beginning, and abode not in the truth, because there is no truth in him. When he speaketh a lie, he speaketh of his own: for he is a liar, and the father of it.

And because I tell you the truth, ye believe me not.

Which of you convinceth me of sin? And if I say the truth, why do ye not believe me?

He that is of God heareth God's words: ye therefore hear them not, because ye are not of God.

Christ never beat around the bush when it came to truth. He told them that they were phonies and never belonged to God. "You are of your father, the devil," he said to them. What a strong and condemning statement. They were no doubt cut to their hearts with these words, and I'm sure they hated him all the more.

What happens to you when you're confronted with the stark truths of scripture? Can't you see that there is a great deal more at stake than just believing when it comes to being born again?

When you believe Christ to the point where you can bow down and worship him as your master and Lord, relinquishing all areas of your life to him, then this is when you'll change. You'll make the transition from being a hearer of the Word, to a doer of the Word: a true disciple.

SO WHAT IMPORTANT TRUTHS HAVE WE LEARNED THUS FAR?

1) That believing Jesus Christ is the son of God is not equal to salvation or being a true disciple of his.
2) That believing Jesus Christ is the Savior of the world is not equal to salvation or being a true disciple of his.

The church has opted to make converts instead of doing what Christ called them to do, which is to make disciples. Granted, it is far easier to make converts than disciples, simply because there is far less effort involved (I'll get to that in a minute). There is another point that I want to make to confirm what I just said. Having been a pastor, I understand that denominations like to compile statistics about such matters. I've completed countless reports over the years that ask very specific questions about the numbers of people who've become converts through our ministry efforts. Never once was I asked how many disciples were made, nor have I ever seen any questions on any of these reports concerning this vital part of ministry, as the Word of God demands. Isn't it amazing that God requires that we make disciples, but the church does not? The church wants to know how many souls were saved and how many of these became members.

A church's reputation or success rises and falls by the reports its pastor sends in. If a church indicates a poor or slightly modest performance in getting souls saved, low growth or loss of membership, or insufficient finances for its size, they're unhappy. To denominations, it's all about good statistics: numbers. They love it when a church does well by the standards they've set. I wonder how they'd feel if they found out they don't measure up to God's standards.

Denominational leadership likes to affirm their satellite church's worth in their organization by favorable statistics. The need to advance the denomination's agenda becomes foremost over preaching the gospel, though they would categorically deny this. Every effort is given to grow at any cost. New programs and entertainment are given priority to draw new people. Service times are shortened to accommodate the busy lifestyles of their congregations, and the message is softened so as not to offend the new folks. Membership loves to support and nurture new programs and outreach with generous financial giving. The church receives accolades from the community for their outreach efforts and being a "team player." The communities support these outreaches as long as God isn't mentioned or preached. Denominational leadership is pleased with the church's great success.

These "Christians" know about Jesus and God, but they'll never become true disciples. They won't be living the dream; they'll be living the lie. The church may grow, but the church pews are filled with dead men's bones: no spiritual life, only death. "Ichabod" could easily be written across the lentil of their church.

1 Samuel 4:21-22

And she named the child Ichabod, saying, The glory is departed from Israel: because the ark of God was taken, and because of her father-in-law and her husband.

And she said, The glory is departed from Israel: for the ark of God is taken.

Be careful of getting easy converts. Winning the lost is not nearly as difficult as churches think. You simply lower the standards for membership. Most Bible-believing churches indicate that they're out "to win the lost at any cost." They start out with good intentions by witnessing in their neighborhoods, hoping to influence even a few. In an effort to appease everyone, some churches even hand out questionnaires to their congregations, asking for suggestions on how the services can be changed to create a friendlier atmosphere. They'll try different approaches but usually discover that getting converts is difficult. When that effort fails, the church pulls out all of the stops, often resorting to gimmicks to get sinners in the doors. They'll claim to do all of this in the name of Christ, of course, to "help grow the church." "Since people like events, let's give them events," they'll say. "We'll worry about getting them saved later," they reason.

Members are anxious for people to see just how friendly everyone is at their church, and they will do almost anything to please new people, to get them there.

Churches eventually resort to proselytizing members of other churches, in their desire to get or keep a piece of the ministry pie. These transplants seldom, if ever, become members, much less disciples of Christ. They're generally disgruntled when they come and disgruntled when they leave. They'll stay for a while but move on to greener pastures, when a hard word or conviction comes.

ILLUSTRATION

I remember, in the past, when gas stations would offer premiums to gain new customers, for example, dinnerware, glasses, stuffed animals, and so on. These new customers were loyal for a while, until they found another free gift gas station. Banks do the same thing today.

HERE ARE SOME OF THE GAMES FOUND IN THE PLAYBOOK:

1) Churches will advertise special dramas or theme-oriented theatrical plays.
2) They will promote youth group activities such as "bring a friend to church" campaigns or community center activities like basketball and baseball.
3) They will advertise various church functions for ladies only, for men only, or for kids only.
4) They will hold special campaigns like feeding and clothing the poor, food collection events, or on-site food pantries.
5) They will bring in famous singing groups for a night or week of entertainment, with a simple salvation message tossed in.
6) They will bring in a well-known evangelist to hold a week of meetings: bring your friends.
7) They will do different types of street ministry.
8) They will offer to provide pickup and delivery services with church vans and buses.
9) They will pass out literature or knock on the doors of everyone around their church to invite them to come.
10) The list goes on and on.

Churches prefer new converts, because it is far simpler and easier to just tell people to believe in Jesus and all of their problems will be over than it is to disciple them in truth.

HERE IS THE REAL TRAGEDY IN ONLY MAKING CONVERTS:

1) Converts never make a difference in the world.
2) Converts never make an impact in the communities in which they live.
3) Converts never make an impact in the churches they attend.
4) Converts never make an impact in the lives of their family members.

But disciples do!

In fact, the disciples actually turned the world upside down for the Kingdom of God. There isn't a single place in scripture referencing the great impact made by early converts. Disciples impacted the world. When converts were made, they were quickly trained by the disciples to be disciples themselves, filled with the Holy Spirit, so they too could impact their world for Christ. And it says in Acts 2:47, "And the Lord added to the church daily such as should be saved."

The church needs to hear this truth and the importance of God's command to go and teach the world, making disciples of them. This is how God's kingdom is to be built here on the earth.

If a true born-again child of God is trained and properly discipled, according to the Word of God, he or she becomes an integral part of the true church of God. Gimmicks are replaced with truth, and new souls are brought to Christ as a matter of course. Remember, intimacy is the only thing that brings forth new life.

Converts need to be trained and properly instructed in the Word of God so that they can be effective as ambassadors for the Kingdom of God, themselves, their communities, their churches, and their own families. To disciple others, you must have the same love for them as Christ does. Making disciples takes time, but it's worth it when you see their life transformed before your very eyes.

A SIMPLE ILLUSTRATION—"TOOLS OF THE TRADE":

There was a time, not that long ago, when mothers would teach their daughters the responsibilities of homemaking. It was done in countless homes throughout America. When these daughters grew up and started families, the process started all over again. It was always mother to daughter; mother to daughter. They simply taught their daughters the things they themselves had been taught. These daughters became disciples of their mothers and were well qualified to teach others.

But then things began changing in our country and it became financially necessary for women to work separately outside the home. Because of this, there wasn't anyone to teach the daughters or sons, so the cycle stopped. Look around and see it for yourself. Now there are very few girls, or young mothers, who even know how to cook or properly care for their families as they once did.

The same thing happened with fathers and sons. As a result, young men no longer take on the responsibilities as the man of the house, to care for their families as God intended. They've become lazy, desiring entertainment over responsibility. They're not taught skills, so they have nothing to teach the next generation.

When the discipleship cycle stops, churches become faultier and ministry stops dead in its tracks. It is little wonder the Christian community is in the condition we are today. We're not a force to be reckoned with in our communities as we once were. Sin is rampant, and our leadership weak. We need to return to our spiritual roots through discipleship. Without it, we have no hope of spiritual recovery.

If you and I will teach the converts the love of God and the basics of salvation, we'll see a resurgence of hope. Joy will fill their hearts, and true ministry will result.

ILLUSTRATION

Oftentimes, when a military commander at a new assignment is confronted with troops that have long been lax because of poor training and discipline, he will set his troops on the road to recovery by returning to the basic principles of soldiering. This takes time, of course, and few enjoy the process, but after a while, they begin see the value in their training and understand that this commander loves them enough to demand change.

We too must return to the basics. "What are these basics?" you ask. They are the truths of scripture, rightly divided by genuine men and women of faith. We need to be taught by those who know and understand the principles of discipleship. If you do not know such people of faith, seek them out. They may not be in your church or even your denomination, but find them and your spiritual life will be better because of it.

Demand that your teachers and pastors reveal the truths of scripture. Ask questions of them, as you compare what they have to say with your own study of God's word. A good pastor or teacher will enjoy the challenge and support your desire to grow spiritually. Start mentoring others when given the opportunity. People longing to know the deep things of God will then seek you out. Make yourself available to them, and then let discipleship begin. It's a natural course. You will love it, and the converts will love you for demanding change.

SOMETHING TO THINK ABOUT:

If the born-again child of God would disciple two people a year, or even one person a year, then the church would double in size every year. Not only that, but the church would be filled with maturing people. New converts will see your changed and committed life and desire to become disciples of Christ themselves. It's a win-win situation. It's how it happened in the early church.

Only disciples will make an impact in your community, people who have a relationship and intimacy with God.

HERE ARE SOME OF THE THINGS YOU, AS A DISCIPLE OF CHRIST, CAN EXPECT:

1) Because of your relationship with Christ, you will know who you really are as a child of God.
2) You will realize freedom from all guilt and condemnation.

3) You will understand the truths of the fourfold ministry of salvation as clearly outlined in scripture:
   a) You'll know with assurance that your sins have been forgiven and cast from you, as far as the east is from the west.
   b) You'll walk in complete and total healing.
   c) You'll understand that you are prosperous and can live in that prosperity while here on the earth.
   d) You'll know that you have been delivered and made free from all things.
4) You are brought to the realization of intimate relationship with the Godhead.
5) You will have constant communication with Almighty God.
6) You will have a covenant with Christ and can now enter boldly into the very throne room of grace at any time.

HERE IS WHAT DISCIPLESHIP REALLY IMPLIES:

1) It means to live a life totally committed to Jesus Christ.
2) It means to make a commitment to seek after and follow the Lord in all issues of life.
3) It means that Christ lives and reigns through you, here on the earth.
4) It means that as a result of your intimacy with Christ, multitudes will witness the true resurrection power of the Lord in your life, desiring it for them.

Being a disciple goes far beyond signing an affirmation card at an altar that says you are born again, or a casual acknowledgment that Christ is the son of God and Savior of the world. It's a lifestyle change and discipleship commitment that transcends human thought, where you are one with Christ, even as he is one with the Father.

True disciples of Christ will avail themselves as mentors to those converts having an "ear to hear" and a "heart to know" the truths of God's word. Patient instruction, planted in good soil, with time, reaps a bountiful harvest.

During discipleship training, converts will learn how to effectively deal with situations because they have been given the mind of Christ at the time of salvation. They will also learn how to handle their emotions so they're not distracted by them in the course of their walk with Christ. They'll also learn how to become doers of the word and not hearers only, learning how to walk in the fullness and completeness of Christ, stating, "As he is, so am I in this world."

THIS IS HOW GOD IS GLORIFIED UPON THE EARTH.

John 12:28-29
Father, glorify thy name. Then came there a voice from heaven, saying, I have both glorified it, and will glorify it again.
The people therefore, that stood by, and heard it, said that it thundered: others said, an angel spake to him.

The Lord speaks to the Father and says, "Father, glorify thy name." The Father, in turn, speaks with an audible voice, saying, "I have glorified it and will glorify it again."

It truly amazes me the lengths that people will go to deny or refuse to believe the things clearly spoken by the Lord. Whether it comes from the pages of scripture, perhaps an audible voice, through miracles or signs and wonders, dreams, or even visitations, many will doubt and argue its authenticity. Doubt comes easily for most people.

The Father speaks, and those around, because of the hardness of their hearts, reject it as not being the voice of the Father at all; some would rather believe an angel spoke. After their rejection of the voice, Jesus tells them that his father's speaking was not for his benefit, but for theirs, and yet they still won't believe because of their hardened hearts.

CONTINUING:

Matthew 28:1-10
In the end of the Sabbath, as it began to dawn toward the first day of the week, came Mary Magdalene and the other Mary to see the sepulchre.

And, behold, there was a great earthquake: for the angel of the Lord descended from heaven, and came and rolled back the stone from the door, and sat upon it.

His countenance was like lightning, and his raiment white as snow: and for fear of him the keepers did shake, and became as dead men.

And the angel answered and said unto the women, fear not ye: for I know that ye seek Jesus, which was crucified.

He is not here: for he is risen, as he said. Come, see the place where the Lord lay.

And go quickly, and tell his disciples that he is risen from the dead; and, behold, he goeth before you into Galilee; there shall ye see him: lo, I have told you.

And they departed quickly from the sepulchre with fear and great joy; and did run to bring his disciples word.

And as they went to tell his disciples, behold, Jesus met them, saying, all hail. And they came and held him by the feet, and worshipped him.

Then said Jesus unto them, be not afraid: go tell my brethren that they go into Galilee, and there shall they see me.

Matthew 28:16
Then the eleven disciples went away into Galilee, into a mountain where Jesus had appointed them.

And when they saw him, they worshipped him: but some doubted.

Jesus's disciples were just told that he had risen. They were instructed to go to a specific place, which they all did. When Jesus appeared to them, they all worshipped him, but it says that some still doubted it was Christ.

It makes you wonder why they even went if they doubted his resurrection in the first place. Perhaps they went out of curiosity, or simply because the other disciples went, hoping their doubt wasn't obvious to those around them.

The disciples weren't sure that it was him. Some were a more skeptical than others, and some just plain didn't believe it was him at all. Later, Thomas, when told that Christ was indeed raised, clearly showed us how far we fall in our doubt. And these were the very people who had followed Jesus during the past three years. They'd witnessed his water baptism by John the Baptist, saw the dove descend, and had even heard the voice of God declaring that Jesus was his only begotten son. During his ministry, they saw the countless miracles, including feeding the multitudes and even his walk on the water. But here in this place, after all of those things, these disciples still doubted or didn't believe at all. They were standing in his presence, staring at his spiritual body; the nail prints in his hands and feet and the place where the spear entered his side, and still doubted.

Friends, we're not far removed from these disciples in our unbelief. Most of us think that it could never happen to us today. We hear the Word of God preached, seeing him clearly through his word. We worship him as God and witness miracles of faith, but there are lingering doubts as to whether any of this is really true. And it's those doubts which cloud our spiritual eyes in unbelief.

When there is a heart of unbelief within an individual, Jesus could walk right into the same room and they would never know it was him. He could even speak to them with calm assuring words, but that wouldn't matter either. Their heart of unbelief would rationalize away the very thing they were witnessing. Most Christians would come up with some logical reason why it wasn't really the truth.

HERE'S AN INTERESTING SCRIPTURE:

John 12:42-43
Nevertheless among the chief rulers also many believed on him; but because of the Pharisees they did not confess him, lest they should be put out of the synagogue: for they loved the praise of men more than the praise of God.

I find this terribly sad. It says "many" believed on him but would not confess him, because they feared the leadership of the church, loving their position more than God.

AND AT THE END OF HIS CONVERSATION WITH THEM, THIS IS WHAT JESUS SAID:

John 8:30
As he spake these words, many believed on him.

John 8:31
Then said Jesus to those Jews which believed on him, if ye continue in my word, then are ye my disciples indeed.

BUT IF WE'RE NOT CHRIST'S DISCIPLES, THEN WHAT IS IT WE REALLY ARE?

John 8:44
Ye are of your father the devil, and the lusts of your father ye will do. He was a murderer from the beginning, and abode not in the truth, because there is no truth in him. When he speaketh a lie, he speaketh of his own: for he is a liar, and the father of it.

OUCH! "THAT'S A BIT HARSH," WOULDN'T YOU SAY?

The words are so pointedly clear. If you are going to follow after Jesus and desire to be true disciples, then you *must* continue in his word. You must follow him and learn his ways. This takes a total commitment and lifestyle change. Are you ready for it?

John 12:42
Nevertheless among the chief rulers also many believed on him; but because of the Pharisees they did not confess him, lest they should be put out of the synagogue.

WHAT DID MANY OF THE CHIEF RULERS BELIEVE?

1) He was the son of God, just like the disciples.
2) He and his father were one, just like the disciples.
3) He was the Messiah, sent by the Father, just like the disciples.
4) He was the nation of Israel's long-awaited Savior, just like the disciples.

In John 8, they also believed they were of Abraham's seed and therefore free. They trusted and believed in their established religion. But they did not confess or trust in him as Messiah and Lord.

There are many scriptures that tell us this sad and tragic story of rejection. Of all the multitudes of people who believed on Jesus while he was here on this earth, very few actually became true disciples. It's no different today.

So call yourself what you like, but if you don't meet the standard of being a true disciple, according to scripture, then you're no better off than the Pharisees and Sadducees. Christ was quite emphatic when he told these religious zealots that their father was the devil. He didn't mince words with them. They preferred to hear how righteous, holy, and important they were to the Kingdom of God. Jesus would have nothing of it. Christ hit the nail squarely on the head with these rulers. As a result of this stinging rebuke, it says they plotted ways to kill him.

What do you think he might be telling the churches today (or you personally)? Has he softened his stand on what a true disciple should be? I don't think so, and I'm sure after reading this book, you do not think so either.

HERE IS ANOTHER POWERFUL SCRIPTURE:

Matthew 10:32-33
Whosoever therefore shall confess me before men, him will I confess also before my father which is in heaven.
But whosoever shall deny me before men, him will I also deny before my father which is in heaven.

I find it tragic that these rulers believed in Jesus as the Christ. They knew scripture, and everything they read pointed directly to him as the long anticipated and glorious Messiah. But they stubbornly rejected him and would not confess him as Lord. These people weren't prepared to submit themselves to his Lordship and follow after him in truth and lifestyle. They rejected the Lord of glory, and it cost them their reward of eternal life.

I can only imagine the terrible threat hanging over the heads of these religious leaders if they were to choose Christ over their coveted position in the synagogue. The mere thought of losing everything, including the position they had fought so long to attain, had to be daunting and foremost on their minds. They also had to understand that they would suffer untold shame and ridicule by their peers or possibly separation from family and friends alike. A decision like this had untold ramifications. But it's a decision that must be made by all. Publicly profess the Lord as Messiah, or keep silent and hope they didn't given their true thoughts and feelings away. We know what happened. They were simply unwilling to risk it all, so they didn't utter a word. The decision cost them dearly.

I believe that there are multitudes of people right here in America today who fit this description. They're not disciples by choice. They have rejected all that Christ is, so he has rejected them. They are not true disciples as they believe or profess, though they often cry out to God in time of need. Their lifestyles give them away.

THIS IS WHAT YOU SEE WHEN YOU LOOK AT THEM:

1) They live a life of denial concerning the revelations of truth.
2) They reject life, and life abundantly, which is in Christ.
3) They have a form of godliness but deny the power thereof.

We don't have the authority to change the criteria for salvation. We only have the authority to preach it and to teach it in truth—making disciples.

The Lord himself has instructed us to make disciples of all nations, teaching them all things that we have been taught, teaching commitment and how to yield and submit to his Lordship.

The word "Christian," simply stated, means "a little Christ." This is a person who walks in his footsteps, lives in his presence, seeks mentoring by the Word of God, and longs to emulate the master. That's a true disciple.

Are you one?

CONCLUSION

DID JESUS DIE IN VAIN?

God poured out his wrath double upon his son, Jesus, when he was crucified. Jesus became the sacrificial lamb on our behalf, punished so that you and I wouldn't be. He died to restore intimacy with God for us, something which no man could ever accomplish on his own, because of his sinful nature.

Since that time, the Father's wrath has been vented; restoration with him is now possible because of Christ's death. God, our Father, hasn't been angry since. Not even once. All the terrible things you see happening around you today and around the world are the result of man's decisions (free will), not God's anger against humanity.

Christ's death was fully sufficient to meet God's demands for the perfect sacrifice, and now we're the recipients of his great love and forgiveness. Intimacy with God is now possible. Everlasting life has been restored to the citizens of earth, to those who would believe.

So, is God still angry? Absolutely not! He loves his creation and wants to restore what sin had destroyed: fellowship and intimacy. He's now focused on drawing and reconciling all men unto himself through his perfect sacrificial gift to mankind: Jesus, the Christ.

2 Corinthians 5:18
And all things are of God, who hath reconciled us to himself by Jesus Christ, and hath given to us the ministry of reconciliation; to wit, that God was in Christ, reconciling the world unto himself, not imputing their trespasses unto them; and hath committed unto us the word of reconciliation.

Now then we are ambassadors for Christ, as though God did beseech you by us: we pray you in Christ's stead, be ye reconciled to God.

For he hath made him to be sin for us, who knew no sin; that we might be made the righteousness of God in him.